Building a Godly Home

Monique Chika Kalu

Building a Godly Home

Copyright © 2016 Monique Chika Kalu

Tel: +234-802-357-2650

Email: passionintensified@gmail.com

ISBN: 9785033732
ISBN-13: 978-978-50337-3-1

Published by Global Reach Publishing LLC

Printed in the United States of America

Understanding Godly home will empower you to live the life God has called you to live, growing in grace, and increasing in wisdom and understanding, by the Spirit, and through the knowledge of God's Word.

CONTENTS

DEDICATION

I dedicate this book to God Almighty.

INTRODUCTION

L ife is beautiful and a Godly home is beautiful as life. It starts with the couple potentially loving themselves as believers, progressively teaching their children the way of the Lord and powerfully propagating the Gospel of our Lord and Savior Jesus Christ to give lives a new meaning.

Potentially, the couple builds their self-concept, understands the rules of relationship and maxims of maturity to have a beautiful marriage.

Progressively, they create a strong family bond where they teach their children the Word of God and train them in the way they should go (*Proverb 22:6*).

Powerfully, the couple builds intimacy in their spiritual life through faith in God. Thereby living the Word of God and doing the right things at the right time and for the right purpose, by the power of the Holy Spirit.

As a child of God and blessed couple, you should build a closer relationship with God; building a strong bond of shared faith that do not just build an extraordinary marital bond but creates the perfect bond of unity among the family members to accomplish God's vision and be totally fulfilled.

A Godly home is a concept that begins with the couple. In other words, the couple must build their self-concept first, and love each other. They should understand the rules of real relationship, what it takes to have a beautiful marriage, especially when it comes to spiritual connection to build a unique family bond and allow God to be in charge of your home.

Get ready for a life changing experience as you explore the glory that is in this masterpiece.

CHAPTER ONE

UNDERSTANDING

GODLY HOME

Building a godly home is a lifestyle that reverences God and manifests love for the Almighty God. It is a way of life where one pursues right standing with God and true goodness; having the loving fear of God and being Christlike, and living a life of prosperity.

Building a godly home is living the good life. It starts with wisdom and its understanding enables you to establish your life, home and family. Lots of people had enough wisdom to start the family, but lacked the understanding to establish it. Understanding godly home will empower you to set it on a firm foundation.

Proverbs 24:3 [AMP] *"Through skillful and godly Wisdom is a house (a life, a home, a family) built, and by understanding it is established [on a sound and good* *foundation],"*

A godly home is more than a fixed place of abode or one's dwelling place. It is an atmosphere of reverence and love that keeps you in God's holy arena where the Word of God becomes the rule of your duty, and duty becomes delight. Understanding godly home is understanding the assurance of the good life God has called you to live.

Deuteronomy 4:40 [AMP] *"Therefore you shall keep His statutes and His commandments, which I command you this day, that it may go well with you and your children after you and that you may prolong your days in the land which the Lord your God gives you forever."*

The Message Bible puts it this way, *"Obediently live by his rules and commands which I'm giving you today so that you'll live well and your children after you —oh, you'll live a long time in the land that* GOD, *your God, is giving you."* (**Deuteronomy 4:40 MSG**).

God has given you a life! He has empowered you to

set your home on a firm foundation also. No matter the level of life where you live, you have been granted the spirit of wisdom and understanding which enables you to deal excellently in the affairs of life. Understanding godly home will empower you to live the life God has called you to live, growing in grace, and increasing in wisdom and understanding, by the Spirit, and through the knowledge of God's Word.

A godly home is a realm in life where you are always eager to live. It is a place where you and your family can live all the way. It is a place to enjoy; a place of abode that is generally pleasing. An excellent place that excites the keenest of the good life to the senses and stirs the higher life beyond the senses. A realm of raving beauty that is always peaceful and welcoming. A godly home is a place to tend and make beautiful. It is a realm of life where you experience the transforming love of Christ and activate a showcase for grace; enjoying the beauty of our God.

The relationship that exists between the people within the godly home is a relationship that glorifies God always. This relationship starts with the couple potentially loving themselves as believers and as Christ loves the church.

Ephesians 5:21-28 [MSG] *"Out of respect for Christ, be courteously reverent to one another. Wives, understand and support your husbands in ways that show your support for Christ. The husband provides leadership to his wife the way Christ does to his church, not by domineering but by cherishing. So just as the church submits to Christ as he exercises such leadership, wives should likewise submit to their husbands. Husbands, go all out in your love for your wives, exactly as Christ did for the church—a love marked by giving, not getting. Christ's love makes the church whole. His words evoke her beauty. Everything he does and says is designed to bring the best out of her, dressing her in dazzling white silk, radiant with holiness. And that is how husbands ought to love their wives.*

They're really doing themselves a favor—since they're already "one" in marriage."

As you can see, an ideally godly home begins with the husband and wife building their self-concept and loving each other in marriage. In other words, it is very important for couple to understand a godly home and what it takes to have a beautiful marriage, especially when it comes to spiritual connection that is needed to nurture a unique love; calling into being a unique family bond that allows God to be in charge of your home. Understanding godly home enables the couple to make God their focus. And when God is the focus of the couple, they draw close to each other in view of the fact that their closeness to God draws them to each other, and empowers then to have a happy and godly home. Understanding godly home is a call that is important as you and beautiful as life. You have a life and it is in your best interest to manifest the beauty of our God. That is why our Lord and Saviour Jesus Christ described marriage on a very spiritual level.

Matthew 19:4-5 [AMP] *"He replied, Have you never read that He Who made them from the beginning made them male and female, And said, For this reason a man shall leave his father and mother and shall be united firmly (joined inseparably) to his wife, and the two shall become one flesh?"*

Godly home is a way of life we have been instructed to live from the beginning. It is so vital that God Almighty gave the instruction at creation in **Genesis 2:24** *"Therefore a man shall leave his father and his mother and shall become united and cleave to his wife, and they shall become one flesh."* (**AMP**)

Therefore, in order to have a godly home, couples should learn to cling to the Lord, *"You shall [reverently] fear the Lord your God; you shall serve Him and cling to Him, and by His name and presence you shall swear."* (**Deuteronomy 10:20 AMP**), hold fast to God's ways, *"For if you diligently keep all this commandment which I command you to do, to love the Lord your God, to* *walk in all His ways, and to cleave to Him—."* (**Deuteronomy 11:22 AMP**), serve God and cling to Him, *"You shall walk after the Lord your God and [reverently] fear Him, and keep His commandments and obey His voice, and you shall serve Him and cling to Him."* (**Deuteronomy 13:4 AMP**), obey God's voice and hold fast to Him, *"And may love the Lord your God, obey His voice, and cling to Him. For He is your life and the length of your days, that you may dwell in the land which the Lord swore to give to your fathers, to Abraham, Isaac, and Jacob."* (**Deuteronomy 30:20**).

There is so much to enjoy when you make God the focus in your home. Looking at the last verse in the above paragraph in the Message Bible, it reads, *"And love GOD, your God, listening obediently to him, firmly embracing him. Oh yes, he is life itself, a long life settled on the soil that GOD, your God, promised to give your ancestors, Abraham, Isaac, and Jacob."* (**Deuteronomy 30:20 MSG**).

As a born-again Christian, Abraham's blessings are

yours! When you were born again, you became the seed of Abraham and thus the inheritor of Abraham's blessings. When you make Christ the center of your home, you establish your home on a firm foundation that can never collapse. This makes your relationship with Christ stronger and makes you the real descendant of Abraham, and therefore the possessor of the blessings God conferred on him.

Galatians 3:29 [MSG] *"Also, since you are Christ's family, then you are Abraham's famous "descendant," heirs according to the covenant promises."*

There are covenant promises which include *"...a long life settled on the soil that GOD, your God, promised to give your ancestors, Abraham, Isaac, and Jacob."* (**Deuteronomy 30:20 MSG**), and *"...that it may go well with you and your children after you and that you may prolong your days in the land which the Lord your God gives you forever."* (**Deuteronomy 4:40 AMP**).

All these blessings are yours; wouldn't you rather have a godly home? As the seed of Abraham, nothing is too good for you. You're blessed beyond measure. As the seed of Abraham, the works of your hands are blessed; you are ordained to succeed. Fruitfulness and productivity have become your birthright. This is your heritage as the seed of Abraham.

The understanding of godly home will empower you to comprehend the truth that you can have a home that reverences and loves God. This consciousness will fill you with the ability to take your place in marriage, knowing that your marriage is blessed with children because a home is made of a man, wife and children.

Establishing your home with God's firm foundation will empower you to exercise your right in Christ. Understanding godly home will enable you to know that it's impossible for you to be barren because Abraham's seed can't be barren.

Deuteronomy 7:14 "*...there shall not be male or female barren among you...*"

In other words, with the consciousness of a godly home, you know you are prospering and living in the manifestation of your infinite blessings in view of the fact that you are Abraham's seed. You are an heir according to the promise and a joint heir with Jesus.

As a man who has grown with the consciousness and truth of a godly home, you know you will get married and *"Your wife shall be like a fruitful vine in the innermost parts of your house; your children shall be like olive plants round about your table."* (**Psalms 128:3 AMP**).

Because you reverently and worshipfully fear the Lord; having a godly home, the blessings are yours. When the Bible refers to your wife being like a fruitful vine in the innermost parts of your house, it means your wife will bear children as a vine bears grapes, your household lush as a vineyard.

Imagine your life, home and family being characterized by abundance just because you built and established a godly home. Deeper understanding of godly home will make you reverence and love God greatly. In a godly home, your wife is fertile and your children are growing vigorously. You do things that are appealing to the senses and thrive greatly beyond the senses.

Psalms 127:3-5 [MSG] *"Don't you see that children are GOD's best gift? the fruit of the womb his generous legacy? Like a warrior's fistful of arrows are the children of a vigorous youth. Oh, how blessed are you parents, with your quivers full of children! Your enemies don't stand a chance against you; you'll sweep them right off your doorstep."*

The Amplified Bible version puts this Rhema this way!

Psalms 127:3-5 [AMP] *"Behold, children are a heritage from the Lord, the fruit of the womb a reward. As arrows, so are the children of one's youth. Happy, blessed, {and} fortunate is the man whose quiver is filled with them. They will not be put to shame when they speak with their adversaries [in gatherings] at the [city's] gate."*

When you have a godly home, you are blessed in the city, you are blessed in the field, you are blessed in your going out and you are blessed in your coming in. it takes a man who has entered into his rest in a godly home to conquer in this busy and wonderful world. A godly home is a beautiful place to enjoy. It is a place of relaxation for you as a man. It is a shield and an insulation from the world and its pressures for the woman. It is a place of refreshing and strengthening for the couple and a place of training for the children.

Every couple can have a godly home! Each and every one of them can establish a lifestyle that enables them to train the fruits of their marriage, their children, to be like them in experiencing the transforming love of Christ, activating a showcase for all-grace and manifesting the beauty of our God. It is absolutely in the man's best interest as the head of the family to make Christ Jesus his head and establish his home on a sound and good foundation. It is very important to establish your home God's way, and do all things right the first time always. It will do you a lot of good to obediently do things in a way to glorify God and His Son, Jesus Christ; acknowledging Him as the head of your home.

Matthew 7:24-25 [MSG] *"These words I speak to you are not incidental additions to your life, homeowner improvements to your standard of living. They are foundational words, words to build a life on. If you work these words into your life, you are like a smart carpenter who built his house on solid rock. Rain poured down, the river flooded, a tornado hit—but nothing moved that house. It was fixed to the rock."*

It is your wisdom to build your house on solid rock, and establish your home on a sound and good foundation. You do not need to struggle through life, trying to work hard. It is OK to follow your dreams but it is better to involve God in your life as a person. It is much more better as a couple to involve God in your lives and dealings so that you do not grow further and further apart living selfishly and unfulfilled. Making God the focus in your life, home and family is the best way to have a happy home because a godly home is a happy home. All you need to do is to acknowledge Christ as the foundation and head of your home.

Luke 6:47-49 [AMP] *"For everyone who comes to Me and listens to My words [in order to heed their teaching] and does them, I will show you what he is like: He is like a man building a house, who dug and went down deep and laid a foundation upon the rock; and when a flood arose, the torrent broke against that house and could not shake or move it, because it had been securely built or founded on a rock. But he who merely hears and does not practice doing My words is like a man who built a house on the ground without a foundation, against which the torrent burst, and immediately it collapsed and fell, and the breaking and ruin of that house was great."*

The Word of God is God's manual for marriage! Lots of people describe marriage as a mystery but it is not a mystery to those who have built their lives, homes and families on the Word. The Word Works! Remember *"Through skilful {and} godly wisdom is a house (a life, a home, a family) built, and by understanding it is established [on a sound and good foundation]."* (**Proverbs 24:3 AMP**).

The word - skilful used in the verse above means a learned power of doing something competently. A godly home does not happen, yes! It does not just happen. You must be a student of the Word; you must give yourself to the Word, learn the Word of God so that you can live the Word and prosper in all things. Continually give yourself to the Word! Delight yourself in the Lord by joyfully acting on the Word and living by it! Be a godly man and have a godly home.

Psalms 1:1-6 [AMP] *"Blessed (happy, fortunate, prosperous, and enviable) is the man who walks and lives not in the counsel of the ungodly [following their advice, their plans and purposes], nor stands [submissive and inactive] in the path where sinners walk, nor sits down [to* relax and rest] where the scornful [and the mockers] gather. But his delight and desire are in the law of the Lord, and on His law (the precepts, the instructions, the teachings of God) he habitually meditates (ponders and studies) by day and by night. And he shall be like a tree firmly planted [and tended] by the streams of water, ready to bring forth its fruit in its season; its leaf also shall not fade or wither; and everything he does shall prosper [and come to maturity]. Not so the wicked [those disobedient and living without God are not so]. But they are like the chaff [worthless, dead, without substance] which the wind drives away. Therefore the wicked [those disobedient and living without God] shall not stand [justified] in the judgment, nor sinners in the congregation of the righteous [those who are upright and in right standing with God]. For the Lord knows and is fully acquainted with the way of the righteous, but the way of the ungodly [those living outside God's will] shall perish (end in ruin and come to nought)."

Isaiah 58:14 "Then shalt thou delight thyself in the LORD; and I will cause thee to ride upon the high places of the *earth, and feed thee with the heritage of Jacob thy father: for the mouth of the LORD hath spoken it."*

It is amazing to know that giving yourself to the Word and having a godly home will empower you to be free to enjoy God. The Message Bible puts it this way *"Then you'll be free to enjoy GOD! Oh, I'll make you ride high and soar above it all. I'll make you feast on the inheritance of your ancestor Jacob."* (**Isaiah 58:14 AMP**) Yes! God says so!

What are you waiting for? Wouldn't you rather give yourself to the Word of God and have a godly home? The Word of God is God's recipe for success. It is the secret to a victorious, successful, struggle-free, lovely home and immeasurable good life. Live in God's Word, by God's Word and through God's Word in this day and age. Activate the good life in its fullness and all-grace you need to prosper in all things; giving yourself totally to the Word.

Have a quiet time with the Lord and ensure you hold regular devotions with your spouse and children. It matters how you train your children; point out to them the right path they must follow. Create a strong family bond! Train your children to know the importance of family worship and attending church services regularly.

Deuteronomy 6:6-9 [MSG] *"Write these commandments that I've given you today on your hearts. Get them inside of you and then get them inside your children. Talk about them wherever you are, sitting at home or walking in the street; talk about them from the time you get up in the morning to when you fall into bed at night. Tie them on your hands and foreheads as a reminder; inscribe them on the doorposts of your homes and on your city gates."*

Proverbs 22:6 [MSG] *"Point your kids in the right direction— when they're old they won't be lost."*

I know you do not want your children to be lost. Make your home a home worthy of the blessings of God. Teach your children to pray effectively and let them know that God answers them when they pray.

Make your house a house of prayer, "...*My house is a house of prayer...*" (**Luke 19:46**). Pray in other tongues and speak in tongues consistently, "...*beloved, building up yourselves on your most holy faith, praying in the Holy Ghost.*" (**Jude 1:20**). Programme your spirit, and lead your home God's way. Pray together as a family; programme yourself for the life of success and dominion.

Create a strong family bond as a couple! Attend church services and be involved in church activities! Always sit together at all times especially in church. Do things that suit your home. Be willing to give up certain interests, plans and preferences for the sake of the home. Do not always insist on your own way; be ready to compromise the healthy way. Learn to humble yourself, "...*for God resisteth the proud, but giveth peace unto the humble.*" (**1 Peter 5:5**). Yes, you have the grace to make your home a godly home. Yes, you have the grace to do all things right the first time and always.

2 Corinthians 9:8 *"And God is able to make all grace abound toward you; that ye, always having all sufficiency in all things, may abound to every good work:"*

You have all the competencies and special skills required for excellence in every good work including having a godly home. You have the skillfully and godly wisdom to build your life, home and family, and the understanding to establish it. The ability of God is made available unto you; learn to be a giver and offer a sacrifice to God. God actually demanded for it in **Exodus 23:15** *"…None shall appear before Me empty-handed"* (*AMP*). As a family, do not go to church empty-handed. Get relevant in the kingdom and make your life count. Lead your life and increase your leadership in your life, home and family. Nothing can be compared to the blessings of the Lord that are present in a godly home. Stand out in this life and make your home outstanding. Encourage yourself in the Lord and be able to say *"…as for me and my house, we will serve the LORD."* (*Joshua 24:15*).

CHAPTER TWO

FINDING AND MARRYING
A GODLY SPOUSE

A godly home is an atmosphere of reverence and love where you, your spouse and family live in God's holy arena; making the Word of God your delight and the rule of your duty. A godly home requires a godly couple! If you really want to have a godly home, you find and marry a godly spouse in view of the fact that the transforming love of Christ and manifestation of all-grace is only possible in a godly home.

The choice to find and marry a wife or husband is a choice you do not make in a hurry. That is why the book of Proverbs emphasizes the need especially for a young man to give thought to his choice of a wife. As a believer, you require maturity and faith in the Word of God to walk this path. It is important for you to be godly and marry a godly spouse. It is in your best interest to consider the choice of a life and godly spouse carefully so that you can live a beautiful life and enjoy a beautiful marriage.

Before we look into finding and marrying a godly spouse, let us skillfully study this wisdom from the book of Proverbs.

Marriage is viewed as a divine institution and it is God who gives a man a virtuous wife.

Proverbs 19:14 [MSG] *"House and land are handed down from parents, but a congenial spouse comes straight from GOD."*

A man's choice of a life's mate can be his making or his breaking, be either a delight or a disaster.

Proverbs 18:22 [AMP] *"He who finds a [true] wife finds a good thing and obtains favor from the Lord."*

It is better to live in a desert land than with a contentious and vexing woman.

Proverbs 21:19 [AMP] *"It is better to dwell in a desert* *land than with a contentious woman and with vexation."*

Proverbs 27:15-16 *"A continual dropping in a very rainy day and a contentious woman are alike. Whosoever hideth her hideth the wind, and the ointment of his right hand, which bewrayeth itself."*

The potential of a wife good or evil is summed up in the words of this proverb *"A virtuous woman is a crown to her husband: but she that maketh ashamed is as rottenness in his bones."* (***Proverbs 12:4***)

As you can see from the study, the decision to marry is a decision that is powerful as life and you cannot afford to make it wrongly.

In the Book of **Genesis,** there is an interesting contrast between the selection of Rebekah as Isaac's wife (*chapter 24*) and Jacob's choice of Rachel, rather than Leah (*chapter 29*). Abraham sent his oldest and most-trusted servant to select a wife for Isaac, within the guidelines he laid down, *"And Abraham said unto his eldest servant of his house, that ruled over all that he* *had, Put, I pray thee, thy hand under my thigh: And I will make thee swear by the LORD, the God of heaven, and the God of the earth, that thou shalt not take a wife unto my son of the daughters of the Canaanites, among whom I dwell: But thou shalt go unto my country, and to my kindred, and take a wife unto my son Isaac."* (**Genesis 24:2-4**). The test which the servant wisely devised, *"Behold, I stand here by the well of water; and the daughters of the men of the city come out to draw water: And let it come to pass, that the damsel to whom I shall say, Let down thy pitcher, I pray thee, that I may drink; and she shall say, Drink, and I will give thy camels drink also: let the same be she that thou hast appointed for thy servant Isaac; and thereby shall I know that thou hast shewed kindness unto my master."*(**Genesis 24:13-14**) was one which revealed the character of the young woman who is a servant at heart and willing to give water to the stranger and his camels.

Jacob, on the other hand, chose a wife for himself. He was unwilling to marry Leah, the older daughter, even though that was the accepted custom in his days (*Genesis 29:26*). Jacob favoured Rachel over Leah, not because of her character, but because of her looks and personality (*Genesis 29:17*). Looking at the things that happened later, one would be convinced to believe that Leah was God's preference while Rachel was Jacob's choice. Leah outlived her younger sister, for example. Leah and her maids bore twice as many children as Rachel and her maiden. Leah bore Judah, the one through whom the Messiah would come, and Levi, the leader of the priestly tribe. It was Leah who was buried in the cave of Machpelah, beside Abraham and Sarah, Isaac and Rebekah (*Genesis 49:31*), while Rachel was buried along the way to Bethlehem (*Genesis 35:19*).

What Genesis teaches us in practice, Proverbs teaches us in principle; a man who would marry well will choose his life's mate on the basis of her character, not on the basis of her looks or her personality.

Proverbs 31:30 [AMP] *"Charm and grace are deceptive,*

and beauty is vain [because it is not lasting], but a woman who reverently and worshipfully fears the Lord, she shall be praised!"

A woman who reverently and worshipfully fears the Lord is a godly spouse and that is the wife every man wants to spend his life with.

You can find and marry a good wife. Yes, you can! I will be teaching you the character traits of a godly wife to empower you to marry and build a godly home. The character of a godly wife to be and in the making is not hidden, when you see, you will definitely know and enjoy the good life.

Proverbs 18:22 *"Whoso findeth a wife findeth a good thing, and obtaineth favour of the LORD."*

A godly wife has a proper relationship with God. She is first and foremost a woman who reverences and loves God.

Proverbs 31:10-31 [MSG] *"A good woman is hard to find, and worth far more than diamonds. Her husband* *trusts her without reserve, and never has reason to regret it. Never spiteful, she treats him generously all her life long. She shops around for the best yarns and cottons, and enjoys knitting and sewing. She's like a trading ship that sails to faraway places and brings back exotic surprises. She's up before dawn, preparing breakfast for her family and organizing her day. She looks over a field and buys it, then, with money she's put aside, plants a garden. First thing in the morning, she dresses for work, rolls up her sleeves, eager to get started. She senses the worth of her work, is in no hurry to call it quits for the day. She's skilled in the crafts of home and hearth, diligent in homemaking. She's quick to assist anyone in need, reaches out to help the poor. She doesn't worry about her family when it snows; their winter clothes are all mended and ready to wear. She makes her own clothing, and dresses in colorful linens and silks. Her husband is greatly respected when he deliberates with the city fathers. She designs gowns and sells them, brings the sweaters she knits to the dress shops. Her clothes are well-made and elegant, and she always faces tomorrow with a smile. When she speaks she has something worthwhile to say, and she always says it kindly. She keeps an eye on everyone in her household, and keeps them all busy and productive. Her children respect and bless her; her husband joins in with words of praise: "Many women have done wonderful things, but you've outclassed them all!" Charm can mislead and beauty soon fades. The woman to be admired and praised is the woman who lives in the Fear-of-GOD. Give her everything she deserves! Festoon her life with praises!"*

A godly wife is wise! She is characterized by wisdom; marked by deep understanding, keen discernment and a capacity for sound judgement. She is prudent, she participates with awareness in everything she does. She has great understanding, unusual discernment and judgement in dealing with affairs of life. She is wisdom personified. She is a woman of wisdom! You will recall that wisdom is personified as a woman in the Book of Proverb.

"Wisdom crieth without; she uttereth her voice in the streets: She crieth in the chief place of concourse, in the

openings of the gates: in the city she uttereth her words, saying, How long, ye simple ones, will ye love simplicity? and the scorners delight in their scorning, and fools hate knowledge? Turn you at my reproof: behold, I will pour out my spirit unto you, I will make known my words unto you. Because I have called, and ye refused; I have stretched out my hand, and no man regarded; But ye have set at nought all my counsel, and would none of my reproof: I also will laugh at your calamity; I will mock when your fear cometh; When your fear cometh as desolation, and your destruction cometh as a whirlwind; when distress and anguish cometh upon you. Then shall they call upon me, but I will not answer; they shall seek me early, but they shall not find me: For that they hated knowledge, and did not choose the fear of the LORD: They would none of my counsel: they despised all my reproof. Therefore shall they eat of the fruit of their own way, and be filled with their own devices. For the turning away of the simple shall slay them, and the prosperity of fools shall destroy them. But whoso hearkeneth unto me shall dwell safely, and shall be quiet from fear of evil." (**Proverbs 1:20-33**)

"Doth not wisdom cry? and understanding put forth her voice? She standeth in the top of high places, by the way in the places of the paths. She crieth at the gates, at the entry of the city, at the coming in at the doors. Unto you, O men, I call; and my voice is to the sons of man. O ye simple, understand wisdom: and, ye fools, be ye of an understanding heart. Hear; for I will speak of excellent things; and the opening of my lips shall be right things. For my mouth shall speak truth; and wickedness is an abomination to my lips. All the words of my mouth are in righteousness; there is nothing froward or perverse in them. They are all plain to him that understandeth, and right to them that find knowledge. Receive my instruction, and not silver; and knowledge rather than choice gold. For wisdom is better than rubies; and all the things that may be desired are not to be compared to it. I wisdom dwell with prudence, and find out knowledge of witty inventions. The fear of the LORD is to hate evil: pride, and arrogancy, and the evil way, and the froward mouth, do I hate. Counsel is mine, and sound wisdom: I am understanding; I have strength. By me kings reign, and princes decree justice. By

me princes rule, and nobles, even all the judges of the earth. I love them that love me; and those that seek me early shall find me. Riches and honour are with me; yea, durable riches and righteousness. My fruit is better than gold, yea, than fine gold; and my revenue than choice silver. I lead in the way of righteousness, in the midst of the paths of judgment: That I may cause those that love me to inherit substance; and I will fill their treasures. The LORD possessed me in the beginning of his way, before his works of old. I was set up from everlasting, from the beginning, or ever the earth was. When there were no depths, I was brought forth; when there were no fountains abounding with water. Before the mountains were settled, before the hills was I brought forth: While as yet he had not made the earth, nor the fields, nor the highest part of the dust of the world. When he prepared the heavens, I was there: when he set a compass upon the face of the depth: When he established the clouds above: when he strengthened the fountains of the deep: When he gave to the sea his decree, that the waters should not pass his commandment: when he appointed the foundations of the earth: Then I was by him, as one brought up with him: and I was daily his delight, rejoicing always before him; Rejoicing in the habitable part of his earth; and my delights were with the sons of men. Now therefore hearken unto me, O ye children: for blessed are they that keep my ways. Hear instruction, and be wise, and refuse it not. Blessed is the man that heareth me, watching daily at my gates, waiting at the posts of my doors. For whoso findeth me findeth life, and shall obtain favour of the LORD. *But he that sinneth against me wrongeth his own soul: all they that hate me love death."* (***Proverbs 8:1-36***)

"Wisdom hath builded her house, she hath hewn out her seven pillars: She hath killed her beasts; she hath mingled her wine; she hath also furnished her table. She hath sent forth her maidens: she crieth upon the highest places of the city, Whoso is simple, let him turn in hither: as for him that wanteth understanding, she saith to him, Come, eat of my bread, and drink of the wine which I have mingled. Forsake the foolish, and live; and go in the way of understanding." (***Proverbs 9:1-6***).

A godly wife is a wise woman who builds her house, *"Lady Wisdom builds a lovely home;"* (**Proverbs 14:1a MSG).**

A godly wife honors her husband! She is always willing to bring good name to her husband and show merited respect to the love of her life. She is an honor personified! Her worth brings respect and fame; she is a symbol of distinction and when she speaks, her words give a guarantee of performance. She is that being married to her husband is the recognition of his right to great respect and to an expression of such recognition.

Proverbs 12:4 *"A virtuous woman is a crown to her husband: but she that maketh ashamed is as rottenness in his bones."*

Proverbs 31:11 *"The heart of her husband doth safely trust in her, so that he shall have no need of spoil."*

A godly wife does not humiliate or harass her husband. She is full of grace and that is why honor is given to her; she is known for her graciousness.

Proverbs 11:16 *"A gracious woman retaineth honour: and strong men retain riches."*

A godly wife is faithful to her husband! She is firm in adherence to the vow she is bound to by duty to fulfil her marriage. A godly wife is at one with her husband and on all fours with the four cornerstones of her marriage. She is a wife who can and maintains sexual purity. She is a woman who is virtuous and excellent, *"Who can find a virtuous woman? for her price is far above rubies."* (**Proverbs 31:10**), in whom her husband has complete trust, *"The heart of her husband doth safely trust in her, so that he shall have no need of spoil."* (**Proverbs 31:11**). She does her husband only good and not evil, *"She will do him good and not evil all the days of her life."* (**Proverbs 31:12**). She teaches her son the virtues of sexual purity, *"Give not thy strength unto women, nor thy ways to that which destroyeth kings."* (**Proverbs 31:3**).

A godly wife is a companion and best friend! She is a

fruitful partner and a woman of wisdom. I encourage you my brother to marry a godly woman and build a godly home.

In the same vein, you too can get hitched to a godly man and live with a good spouse; building a godly home today.

In this day and age when it seems like it is very difficult to find a young, decent and faithful man; there is hope for you my sister. Your labour of love will not go unrewarded. Yes, you will marry a man who has the qualities that make a good and godly man.

It is important for you as a young lady to take your time to look out for the traits in your future life partner that will, indeed, shape and make your marriage beautiful. A godly man is surely the man you need and desire.

I know you have prayed as a matured believer and I want you to know that God has answered your prayer for a godly man and a godly home. You are the reason for this book. I wrote this book so that you can have full and complete focus on fulfilling your godly purpose.

You can find a godly man who is very perfect for you. You can marry a godly man and build a godly home with him.

A godly husband loves God! His passion for God manifests in everything he does. Looking at his way of life will compel you to serve God with all your heart because of the love that He has shown you through salvation. He is the kind of man you want to celebrate always. He is a man who has the capacity to love you as Christ loves the church.

1 John 2:16 *"For all that is in the world, the lust of the flesh, and the lust of the eyes, and the pride of life, is not of the Father, but is of the world."*

A godly husband is a man you can have to hold and to keep. He has a complete commitment to building the kingdom of God. He loves witnessing to the lost and cares for those in need. His tender heart if a perfect reflection of God's love.

2 Timothy 4:5 *"But watch thou in all things, endure afflictions, do the work of an evangelist, make full proof of thy ministry."*

A godly spouse is a giver! He is known for his generosity; willing to sacrifice his own money, time and energy for others. He is a husband who has securely entrusted his gifts to God and is willing at all times to show great appreciation to you as his wife.

Matthew 6:21 *"For where your treasure is, there will your heart be also."*

A godly husband is a man who is willing to put others before himself. He does not demonstrate an unselfish attitude. He is not a man who wants things to go his way always.

1 Corinthians 10:24 *"Let no man seek his own, but every man another's wealth."*

A godly husband is a man who sets aside his own desires for you, his wife without making you feel guilty about it. He is a perfect reflection of God's grace in everything he says and does.

A godly husband is a man who is experiencing the transforming love of Christ; he is a showcase for grace and the beauty of God. He is a son of consolation! One shoes service to the church is life-giving.

2 Corinthians 9:12 *"For the administration of this service not only supplieth the want of the saints, but is abundant also by many thanksgivings unto God;"*

He is committed to the things of God, especially to God's business of soul winning.

A good husband is one who does the Word! He delights himself to the Word of God. He has made the Word the rule of duty and duty has become his delight. He lives the Word daily!

James 1:22 *"But be ye doers of the word, and not hearers* *only, deceiving your own selves."*

A godly husband is a man who prays fervently and effectively. His intensity and faithfulness in prayer is inspiring! His prayers are heartfelt, meaningful and genuine to the Lord. When he prays and speaks in other tongues, it builds up God's awesome presence in those around him irrespective of what they are going through.

James 5:16 *"Confess your faults one to another, and pray one for another, that ye may be healed. The effectual fervent prayer of a righteous man availeth much."*

A godly husband is a man who is dead to sin and alive in Christ.

Romans 12:2 *"And be not conformed to this world: but be ye transformed by the renewing of your mind, that ye may prove what is that good, and acceptable, and perfect, will of God."*

A godly husband is a man who has good relationship with his family. He knows the importance of family and cherishes family time. He is a man who treats his mother with respect and treats you with super respect as well. He does not speak to his parents disrespectfully or with dishonour. He is a man of purpose and integrity.

1 Peter 5:4 *"And when the chief Shepherd shall appear, ye shall receive a crown of glory that fadeth not away."*

A godly husband relates with other Christians.

Acts 2:24 *"Whom God hath raised up, having loosed the pains of death: because it was not possible that he should be holden of it."*

He is a good man who knows how to communicate, have fun and live on God's Word. He understands the real purpose and importance of marriage. He respects human life and honours femininity. He is a selfless man who is faithful, and can encourage your children to grow in the fear of God.

Whether you are a man or woman, you can find and marry a godly spouse, and build a godly home together. Go ahead and take your place in marriage, and take up your duty; building a godly home.

CHAPTER THREE

TAKING UP YOUR DUTY
AS A GODLY HUSBAND

The word *"husband"* comes from some Anglo-Saxon words which mean **"house band."** This implies a strip of metal (*or rope*) used to bind the house together. A husband therefore binds together the home in terms of its organisation and control.

Looking at the above definition, a godly husband is one who binds his house (*life, home, family*) together, and creates an atmosphere of reverence and love that keeps every member of the house in God's holy arena where the Word of God becomes the rule of duty and duty becomes delight.

A godly husband is a kind of husband every woman aspires to marry. He is an understanding, kind and warm man who is always positive and friendly, not only to his wife and children but also to everyone he comes in contact with. He does not have an inordinate self-esteem and disdainful behaviour. He is a man who is always full of faith, steadfast in affection and firm in adherence to promises or observance of duty.

A godly husband is a man of honour and integrity; a husband that a wife can trust any day, any time. He is a man his wife can count on in all circumstance. He supports his wife in the good and bad times. He cares for his wife and does not speak harshly to his wife. He does not belittle, strike or humiliate her either in public or in private. He listens to her empathetically even when she airs her views on some mutual issues.

A godly husband communicates with his wife; he is honest and open to her at all times. He finds quality time to sit close to his wife, talking on issues from the most trivial to the most serious. He loves his wife and shows affection. He appreciates and notices physical and emotional occurrences in the life of his wife. He does his best and strives to make his wife happy even in bed. He sits on the driver's seat of his marriage, driving the wheels with good love-making as a very essential oil that lubricates.

A godly husband is more than a man! He has duties which he must perform in order to bind his life, home and family together. Becoming a godly husband is a calling which you must fulfil. It is a calling to be not just the head of your life, but also the head of your home and family. It is a way of life where you make right decisions the first time and always. It is a call to responsibility where you do not fail so that you do not blame anyone else when things go wrong. You must have authority in bringing up children and leadership in providing direction and guidance.

You are called to a life of faith and you must be full of faith. You must be steadfast in affection to your spouse and allegiance to the God-head. You must always remember your marital vows to your wife and make your love for God the first and foremost in your life. You must be firm in adherence to promises or in observance of duty. You have a duty! You have duties which you must take up and perform with excellence as a Godly husband.

You are the head of your family and it is in your best interest to make God your Head.

1 Corinthians 11:3 *"But I would have you know, that the head of every man is Christ; and the head of the woman is the man; and the head of Christ is God."*

As the head of your family, it is in your place to provide good leadership to yourself, home and family, your wife wants to know who you are, where you are going, and to know how you are going to get there. It is therefore in your best interest to have confidence in yourself, in your wife, and in your marriage. Lead your life, lead your wife and your children with kindness and understanding. Be firm, yet gentle, do not be proud to consult the Lord and your wife before making any major decision. If you really want to be a successful, and godly husband and father, you must learn to submit yourself to the authority of God the Father and of Jesus Christ His

Son so that you can be able to have authority in bringing up your children. Nothing means so much to a wife who has security and freedom from a husband who is willing, able and capable of taking the lead in the marital relationship she has with him. Be a godly man who uses wisdom to lead his family, not muscle. Lead your wife with compassion and kindness, with a flexibility and desirability that is pleasing to her and bring smiles to the faces of your gorgeous gifts. Always be a godly leader who exhibits stillness, maturity and determination to follow the will of God for yourself all the way.

Ephesians 5:23-24 [MSG] *"Wives, understand and support your husbands in ways that show your support for Christ. The husband provides leadership to his wife the way Christ does to his church, not by domineering but by cherishing. So just as the church submits to Christ as he exercises such leadership, wives should likewise submit to their husbands."*

It is very important for you to take charge and take

up your duty as a godly husband; cherishing your wife. Show your wife love and affection, treat her in a special way so that she can give you herself wholly and sincerely. Give her the best the first time and always. It if means giving your best to her sacrificially, do it and present her back to yourself accordingly. Nourish, cherish and beautify your wife with the Word of God and romantic gifts. Make your wife feel loved, appreciated, wanted and accepted.

Ephesians 5:25-33 [MSG] *"Husbands, go all out in your love for your wives, exactly as Christ did for the church—a love marked by giving, not getting. Christ's love makes the church whole. His words evoke her beauty. Everything he does and says is designed to bring the best out of her, dressing her in dazzling white silk, radiant with holiness. And that is how husbands ought to love their wives. They're really doing themselves a favor—since they're already "one" in marriage. No one abuses his own body, does he? No, he feeds and pampers it. That's how Christ treats us, the church, since we are part of his body. And this is why a man leaves father and mother and cherishes* *his wife. No longer two, they become "one flesh." This is a huge mystery, and I don't pretend to understand it all. What is clearest to me is the way Christ treats the church. And this provides a good picture of how each husband is to treat his wife, loving himself in loving her, and how each wife is to honor her husband."*

Treat your wife very well! Encourage her to be optimistic at all times. Increase her state of well-being and make her feel happy at home.

Ecclesiastes 9:9 [AMP] *"Live joyfully with the wife whom you love all the days of your vain life which He has given you under the sun—all the days of futility. For that is your portion in this life and in your work at which you toil under the sun."*

Proverbs 5:18 [AMP] *"Let your fountain [of human life] be blessed [with the rewards of fidelity], and rejoice in the wife of your youth."*

Let her feel accepted and special! Stay at home with her as often as possible and provide a fellowship that is an outgrowth of a lovely companionship. Do not talk to her anyhow and do not take advantage of your wife.

Colossians 3:19 [MSG] *"Husbands, go all out in love for your wives. Don't take advantage of them."*

It is important to listen to your wife a lot and encourage her to talk. Aside from the fact that she wants to talk to you, she sees it as a form of your respect to her. She wants to feel important with you especially when both of you are outside. Talk about your wife positively all the time and be patient with her as she grows with you because she is a weaker vessel.

1 Peter 3:7 [AMP] *"In the same way you married men should live considerately with [your wives], with an intelligent recognition [of the marriage relation], honoring the woman as [physically] the weaker, but [realizing that you] are joint heirs of the grace (God's unmerited favor) of life, in order that your prayers may not be hindered and cut off. [Otherwise you cannot pray effectively.]"*

Show your wife honor! Think highly of her, look up to her, have polite regard for her and be thoughtful of her; showing her kind consideration and concern. Your wife is tender; she deserves a tender and loving care. It may not be in your best interest to criticize your wife or defend yourself. Touch her at the right places, compliment her, smile and laugh with her without exception. Respect your wife and always respect the private moments you shared together. Be confident and respect your wife, it helps her to function well.

Psalms 34:11-14 *"Come, ye children, hearken unto me: I will teach you the fear of the LORD. What man is he that desireth life, and loveth many days, that he may see good? Keep thy tongue from evil, and thy lips from speaking guile. Depart from evil, and do good; seek peace, and pursue it."*

Ephesians 5:33 *"Nevertheless let every one of you in particular so love his wife even as himself; and the wife see that she reverence her husband."*

Be a good husband to your wife. Protect her form the strain of house chores. Protect your wife from the attacks of relatives and friends. Your wife is more open, subject or unresistant to some stimulus and influence such as attacks, especially psychological and emotional attacks. And it is in your best interest to protect her from these attacks. It is your wisdom to understand your wife and help her to organise her life the right way with course of actions that produce results.

1 Peter 3:7 [MSG] *"The same goes for you husbands: Be good husbands to your wives. Honor them, delight in them. As women they lack some of your advantages. But in the new life of God's grace, you're equals. Treat your wives, then, as equals so your prayers don't run aground."*

A godly husband is a family! Yes, he is and you are a family man. It is true that raising a family takes hard work but you really need to work smart because children need the kind of father they can trust and the kind of father who trust the Lord. Give your children legacy! Do not just exist, live for a purpose. Make your home a place of peace, security, respect and harmony. Do all you can to encourage and enforce family value in your home and family. Do not talk the wrong way and do not do things that devalue your personality and marriage; degrading your children is not in your best interest, train them well.

Proverbs 22:6 *"Train up a child in the way he should go: and when he is old, he will not depart from it."*

One of the indispensable traits that will enable you to take up your duty as a godly husband is maturity. Maturity means growing in awareness of others and the world around you. Growing in maturity as a godly husband means growing and participating in awareness with respect to your life, home and family. It is your wisdom not to go into debt; do all you can to have peace of mind always and all the way. Be satisfied with your spending plan, and set goals for your future that will help build a strong marriage and an example for your children to follow in their own lives. Plan your budget and do not spend beyond your means; don't make your want your goals. You must provide food, accommodation, clothing, education, insurance and spiritual comfort through the Word of God, prayer and church.

1 Timothy 5:8 [GW] *"If anyone doesn't take care of his own relatives, especially his immediate family, he has denied the Christian faith and is worse than an unbeliever."*

In fact, a godly husband is a man who provides for his families, not just his family. When you do this, you are enabling your wife to become a wife who appreciates and supports.

1 Timothy 5:8 *"But if any provide not for his own, and specially for those of his own house, he hath denied the faith, and is worse than an infidel."*

Proverbs 31:11-12 *"The heart of her husband doth safely trust in her, so that he shall have no need of spoil. She will do him good and not evil all the days of her life."*

Make your wife your best friend! Listen to her and pray with her; it enables you to become more powerful and empowers her to be more beautiful. It is important for you to know that genuine love and sharing of ideas are not defined by an emotional experience. Knowing your spouse's motivation, thoughts or ways is very important. Do not encourage conflict in your home and family; be devoted and matured. Always long to talk to your wife about everything. Learn to communicate with your sweetheart in view of the fact that your marriage will wither and become dry just like the soul when it has no time with God. Learn to give argument a miss! Talk quality and not quantity talk. Think about the things you must talk about before you voice them out. It is wisdom to know the right thing to say at the right time and for the right purpose.

Proverbs 23:15-16 *"My son, if thine heart be wise, my heart shall rejoice, even mine. Yea, my reins shall rejoice, when thy lips speak right things."*

When you talk, be honest. Truthfulness and honesty are absolutes in life, and they must never be compromised. Refuse to tell lies, cheat or deceive your wife in any way. Be willful to show fairness and sincerity all the way. No matter where you find yourself along the way, be genuine and give your wife a sense of security. It will not favor you when you get into the business of not keeping an honest and open communication with your wife. It won't be wrong to say that your wife is life; she is your wisdom to live. Make honesty your foundation stone in marriage, do your best to contribute honesty to your marital relationship and build a godly home. Talk with your wife about everything, share your dreams with your wife. Be dedicated with your purpose, pursue your passion. Be responsible for what you think, feel and do. Energize yourself to live above your fear and desire a better achievement. Increase your ability to make a success and motivate yourself towards enhancing your skills and celebrating your possibilities. Do not be manipulated by ego, be confident and increase trust so that you can inspire your wife to become a woman of compassion, encouragement and honor.

Hebrews 13:18 [GW] *"Pray for us. We are sure that our consciences are clear because we want to live honorably in every way."*

1 Peter 2:11, 12 [MSG] *"Friends, this world is not your home, so don't make yourselves cozy in it. Don't indulge your ego at the expense of your soul. Live an exemplary life among the natives so that your actions will refute their prejudices. Then they'll be won over to God's side and be there to join in the celebration when he arrives."*

Live an exemplary life and be loyal to your wife. Do not think of having an affair with another woman and do not have an affair with the strange woman. Be steadfast in affection and make her trust you wholeheartedly. It is important for you to know that if you keep your marital vows, you will keep your marital relationship. Yearn to be firm in adherence to the promises you made on your wedding day and observance of duty in your life, home and family. Be committed to your marriage for the long haul. Be a loyal husband and value your wife. Learn to listen to all of her, let her know she is very important, satisfy her always, hold her and tell her you love her all the way. Learn to communicate your needs and desires to your wife so that she can have the favourable occasion to meet every of your needs. Wouldn't you rather make your intimate time together precious and pure?

Proverbs 20:6-7 *"Most men will proclaim every one his own goodness: but a faithful man who can find? The just man walketh in his integrity: his children are blessed after him."*

You can be a blessing from God to your wife. Yes, you can have a relationship that is truly blessed and a marital relationship that is consecrated and holy. You can live in an atmosphere of reverence and love that keeps you in God's holy arena where the Word of God becomes the rule of duty and duty becomes delight. There is never a doubt of loyalty in this atmosphere. A godly home is an atmosphere of faithfulness! A godly husband lives the Word and does the Word, increasing rust always and all the way.

Proverbs 20:6-7 [AMP] *"Many a man proclaims his own loving-kindness and goodness, but a faithful man who can find? The righteous man walks in his integrity; blessed (happy, fortunate, enviable) are his children after him."*

Be a wise husband who knows that your wife has a need and that need must be satisfied. Understand that your wife also has sexual needs. Be your wife's best friend! Love her and make your marriage work well! Understand your wife and be patient with her. Do not be in a hurry to satisfy her, take your time and maximize the quality time both of you have together. It is better to be patient, don't panic, and plan your future together with confidence than being moved by the things the eyes can see. It is in your favour to do things right always and be a better person who make his wife to feel the way of true love.

Be smart and creative! Generate a love so deep that if sex were not possible for whatever reason, love would still grow. Grow with your wife! Create the necessary environment for a good marriage and godly home. Give attention to making your wife happier and make her feel great at all times.

Song of Solomon 8:6-7 *"Set me as a seal upon thine heart, as a seal upon thine arm: for love is strong as death; jealousy is cruel as the grave: the coals thereof are coals of fire, which hath a most vehement flame. Many waters cannot quench love, neither can the floods drown it: if a man would give all the substance of his house for love, it would utterly be contemned."*

What are you thinking about? What are you waiting for? Wouldn't you rather be a godly husband and a godly man? You can be a godly man and husband; enjoying God's greater blessings.

Titus 2:11-14 [AMP] *"For the grace of God (His*

unmerited favor and blessing) has come forward (appeared) for the deliverance from sin and the eternal salvation for all mankind. It has trained us to reject and renounce all ungodliness (irreligion) and worldly (passionate) desires, to live discreet (temperate, self-controlled), upright, devout (spiritually whole) lives in this present world, Awaiting and looking for the [fulfillment, the realization of our] blessed hope, even the glorious appearing of our great God and Savior Christ Jesus (the Messiah, the Anointed One), Who gave Himself on our behalf that He might redeem us (purchase our freedom) from all iniquity and purify for Himself a people [to be peculiarly His own, people who are] eager and enthusiastic about [living a life that is good and filled with] beneficial deeds."

Be kind to your children! Be a faithful and spiritual leader. Be a family man, a provider, an honest person, a good communicator; a happy husband and loving father. Be your son's first hero and your daughter's first love. Recreate your world and renew your mind! Fix your mind on the Word so that you can teach your children the right ways and precepts. Make your marriage a reflection of God's very best; it is the best life to live as a godly man and husband.

Jeremiah 9:23-24 [MSG] *"Don't let the wise brag of their wisdom. Don't let heroes brag of their exploits. Don't let the rich brag of their riches. If you brag, brag of this and this only: That you understand and know me. I'm GOD, and I act in loyal love. I do what's right and set things right and fair, and delight in those who do the same things. These are my trademarks." GOD's Decree."*

CHAPTER FOUR

TAKING UP YOUR DUTY
AS A GODLY WIFE

Proverbs 3:13-19 *"Happy is the man that findeth wisdom, and the man that getteth understanding. For the merchandise of it is better than the merchandise of silver, and the gain thereof than fine gold. She is more precious than rubies: and all the things thou canst desire are not to be compared unto her. Length of days is in her right hand; and in her left hand riches and honour. Her ways are ways of pleasantness, and all her paths are peace. She is a tree of life to them that lay hold upon her: and happy is every one that retaineth her. The Lord by wisdom hath founded the earth; by understanding hath he established the heavens."*

Proverbs 18:22 *"Whoso findeth a wife findeth a good thing, and obtaineth favour of the Lord."*

Proverbs 19:14 *"House and riches are the inheritance of fathers: and a prudent wife is from the Lord."*

Proverbs 24:3-5 *"Through wisdom is an house builded; and by understanding it is established: And by knowledge shall the chambers be filled with all precious and pleasant riches. A wise man is strong; yea, a man of knowledge increaseth strength."*

Proverbs 31:10 *"Who can find a virtuous woman? for her price is far above rubies."*

Proverbs 31:11 *"The heart of her husband doth safely trust in her, so that he shall have no need of spoil."*

Proverbs 31:18 *"She perceiveth that her merchandise is good: her candle goeth not out by night."*

Proverbs 31:25 *"Strength and honour are her clothing; and she shall rejoice in time to come."*

Proverbs 31:26 *"She openeth her mouth with wisdom; and in her tongue is the law of kindness."*

Proverbs 31:30 *"Favour is deceitful, and beauty is vain: but a woman that feareth the LORD, she shall be praised."*

WOW! What a description. From the truth above, you

will observe that a godly wife is among all, a woman to be admired and praised because she lives in the fear of God. She is a woman who reverently and worshipfully fears the Lord. She knows that building a godly home is a way of life that reverences God and manifests love for the Almighty. She sees through an atmosphere of reverence and love that keeps her life, home and family in God's holy arena where the Word of God becomes the rule of duty and duty becomes delight.

A godly wife is a special being who loves the Lord fervently and can generate a love so deep for her husband. She is her husband's helpmeet. In order words, she is a helper, motivator, uplifter and promoter to her husband. It is very for a wife to be godly and love her husband in view of the fact that it is the easiest way for her to perform her marital responsibilities.

Titus 2:4 [AMP] *"So that they will wisely train the young women to be sane and sober of mind (temperate,* *disciplined) and to love their husbands and their children."*

Ephesians 5:22-24 *"Wives, submit yourselves unto your own husbands, as unto the Lord. For the husband is the head of the wife, even as Christ is the head of the church: and he is the saviour of the body. Therefore as the church is subject unto Christ, so let the wives be to their own husbands in every thing."*

1 Peter 3:1-3 [NIV] *"Likewise, ye wives, be in subjection to your own husbands; that, if any obey not the word, they also may without the word be won by the conversation of the wives; While they behold your chaste conversation coupled with fear. Whose adorning let it not be that outward adorning of plaiting the hair, and of wearing of gold, or of putting on of apparel;"*

Taking up your duty as a godly wife is the fulfilment of your major holy calling. The Bible teaches clearly that wives should submit to their husbands. Godly wives will do well to obey this truth. It is your wisdom as a godly wife to submit to your husband because it is in obedience to the Word of God. It is to bring the lost to the saving knowledge of Jesus Christ and to be precious in the eyes of God.

Taking up your duty as a godly wife is a special mandate. You must learn to capitulate to your husband's desires, surrender to his will, give yourself to him and acquiesce to his lead. You must be champing at the bit to submit always to your husband. Resisting your husband's will is disobeying God. You are not called to act on your will but to condition your heart to love your husband.

Your husband is your head and you must respect him and acknowledge his calling as the high priest of your life, home and family. You must respond to his leadership, praise him, be unified with him in purpose, and in will. You must be a helpmeet to him; listen to him, bless him and be thankful to God for him.

You are a godly wife and you must be an example to the body of Christ. You must live a life of reverence and keep your home so that other women especially the younger women will learn from you.

Titus 2:3-5 [GW] *"Tell older women to live their lives in a way that shows they are dedicated to God. Tell them not to be gossips or addicted to alcohol, but to be examples of virtue. ⁴ In this way they will teach young women to show love to their husbands and children, ⁵ to use good judgment, and to be morally pure. Also, tell them to teach young women to be homemakers, to be kind, and to place themselves under their husbands' authority. Then no one can speak evil of God's word."*

Make your home and keep your home! Be a committed homemaker who is not busy to know that the way to her husband's heart is through his stomach. There is something about washing your hands very well to cook very delicious meals for your husband. Food is every man's delight; it is very important to your husband. It is your duty to cook good and yummy meals for your husband and the rest of your household. You should introduce a lot of variety in the food you prepare. You must learn and master the art of cooking! You must learn to cook and do it properly. It is in your best interest to be creative at putting your knowledge and experience to work. Be innovative and introduce a lot of variety. It is a good thing for a man to come home and have a tasty food to eat.

Song of Solomon 2:5 [MSG] *"Oh! Give me something refreshing to eat—and quickly! Apricots, raisins—anything. I'm about to faint with love! His left hand cradles my head, and his right arm encircles my waist!"*

In this day and age, a lot is required of you as a godly wife. As a godly wife, you are not just a wife; you are a follower of Christ, a worker, a mother, a love-making partner, a cook, a homekeeper and a hostess. You are a super being, you are not ordinary.

As a Christian, you must pray effectively, study the Word of God voraciously, have fellowship with fellow believers, attend church services and be involved in church activities. As a worker, you must put in your best and attain good results in all you do. As a mother, you must be loving and patient, you must be prepared to talk with your children and help out with homework.

As a cook, you must produce good food always with variety and zeal. You must ensure that you adjust to your husband's work schedule, no matter how *"ungodly"* his hours of eating may be. As much as you can, serve your husband yourself and sit by him to keep him company even if you have had your meal earlier. As a homekeeper, you must tidy your home and keep it clean, not only for visitors but for your husband and children as well.

You are not ordinary! You are a godly wife, and godly mother. You are a supermom! You are an exemplary mother, a woman who performs the traditional duties of housekeeping and child rearing while also having a full-time job.

You are beautiful and intelligent! You are like Abigail in the Bible, *"...Abigail; she was a woman of good*

understanding, and beautiful…" (**1 Samuel 25:3 AMP**).
You are the perfect manifestation of a true wife the
Bible described in **Proverbs 18:22** (*AMP*) *"He who
finds a [true] wife finds a good thing and obtains favor
from the Lord."*

You are a true wife and a good spouse! Your husband
found a good life when he found you. Empower him
to enjoy the uniqueness of the good thing he has
found. Be eager and ready at all times to meet his
needs and you own. Offer yourself truly and wholly.
No one has the right to satisfy your husband sexually
except you. Satisfying your husband's sexual needs is
your God-given duty. It is true that the need to make
love is greater for a man than for a woman but it is
acceptable for you to initiate love-making sometimes.
It is in your best interest to do your God-given duty
and satisfy your husband sexually at home. Satisfying
your husband is a duty you can perform completely
and graciously; start with the power of your touch.

Song of Solomon 1:12 *"While the king sitteth at his*

table, my spikenard sendeth forth the smell thereof."

Feel free to tell your husband how much you love him. There is so much you can do to make him confirm your love for him. When he is at work, you can call him to find out how his day is going or even send him an SMS with a simple message – *"I Love You."* Sincerely take your place in your marriage and enjoy the uniqueness of a blissful marriage.

Song of Solomon 1:7 *"Tell me, O thou whom my soul loveth, where thou feedest, where thou makest thy flock to rest at noon: for why should I be as one that turneth aside by the flocks of thy companions?"*

Provide nice supportive company and friendship to your husband. Be smart to chat with him and encourage him. Your encouragement means so much to your husband. Always tell him that you are proud of him and what he does. Admire him all the way and do your very best to make him know that he is your king and a success. Make him feel important and praise him without exception.

Song of Solomon 4:7 *"Thou art all fair, my love; there is no spot in thee."*

It is in your best interest to stand out and be outstanding, taking up your duty as a godly wife. There is something you really need to know, every man accepts as Gospel that he is created for the best and he expects nothing but the best from you. He wants to date a mate who has created her sphere of influence, so that he can recreate his world excellently. Your husband wants you to be a woman of moral virtue, because he knows you are a good and virtuous woman.

Proverbs 31:10-31[TLB] *"If you can find a truly good wife, she is worth more than precious gems! Her husband can trust her, and she will richly satisfy his needs. She will not hinder him but help him all her life. She finds wool and flax and busily spins it. She buys imported foods brought by ship from distant ports. She gets up before dawn to prepare breakfast for her household and plans the day's work for her servant girls. She goes out to inspect a field* *and buys it; with her own hands she plants a vineyard. She is energetic, a hard worker, and watches for bargains. She works far into the night! She sews for the poor and generously helps those in need. She has no fear of winter for her household, for she has made warm clothes for all of them. She also upholsters with finest tapestry; her own clothing is beautifully made—a purple gown of pure linen. Her husband is well known, for he sits in the council chamber with the other civic leaders. She makes belted linen garments to sell to the merchants. She is a woman of strength and dignity and has no fear of old age. When she speaks, her words are wise, and kindness is the rule for everything she says. She watches carefully all that goes on throughout her household and is never lazy. Her children stand and bless her; so does her husband. He praises her with these words: "There are many fine women in the world, but you are the best of them all!" Charm can be deceptive and beauty doesn't last, but a woman who fears and reverences God shall be greatly praised. Praise her for the many fine things she does. These good deeds of hers shall bring her honor and recognition from people of importance."*

Always have the right relationship with God and truly reverence Him. Be a wife your husband can trust and empower your husband to be a man who lacks nothing (*Proverbs 31:10*). Be a helpful wife who gives her husband a shot in the arm to do all things right (*Proverbs 31:12*). Be skilful! Motivate yourself greatly, be industrious, resourceful and trustworthy in everything you do (*Proverbs 31:13,14*). Rise up early in the morning to pray and work (*Proverbs 31:15*). Be a good planner, be wise and productive (*Proverbs 31:16*). Do not be like those who are lazy. Do all you can to tidy and clean your home, not just for visitors but for your husband and children as well (*Proverbs 31:17*). Be wise to help your husband financially when it is possible (*Proverbs 31:18*). Do not be the devil's workshop, do something outstanding (*Proverbs 31:19*). Be kind and do not drive away visitors. Be as hospitable as possible. Be a friend to your husband's friends. Build a great asset that welcomes people to your home; be a cheerful and a happy wife (*Proverbs 31:20*). It is important to dress in view of the fact that the way you dress matters. Be diligent and courteous to dress very well and let your raving beauty keep your husband close to you always (*Proverbs 31:22*). Wash your husband's clothes, ensure he is neat and presentable at all times (*Proverbs 31:23*). Fill yourself with skillful and godly wisdom. Do not be good at habitually finding fault incessantly and do not be a source of persistent annoyance and distraction to any quarters, let your words edify (*Proverbs 31:26*).

It is very important got you as a godly wife to take up your duty. Do not be unoccupied or unemployed, having no evident lawful means to support your husband. Do not spend your time doing nothing and do not be a person that moves lazily or without purpose. Do not idle the day away, this day and age is the time of achievement; therefore, it is in your best interest to cease to pass your time in idleness and do not be idled by anything. Be characterized by peculiarity and have quality that can be described as a perfect form of idiosyncrasy.

Don't try to be like others! Risk it, be different. Do things differently and be distinctively different in all you do. Be wise not to give yourself to talking in a way that devalues you. Talk is not cheap, do not waste your strength of purpose and do not live an empty life. There is more to life and there is so much you can do, being a godly wife, you are worthy, industrious, favoured and empowered. You are not ordinary! You were created to fulfil extraordinary purpose. Even if you make up your mind to be an officious or inquisitive person, don't just do a busy work but be at work with productivity and increase your personality positively, *"She looks well to how things go in her household, and the bread of idleness (gossip, discontent, and self-pity) she will not eat."* **(Proverbs 31:27 AMP)**

Learn to be happy always and anticipate only the best

to happen all the way and minimize all other possibilities. Learn to celebrate your possibilities.

Proverbs 17:22 [AMP] *"A happy heart is good medicine and a cheerful mind works healing, but a broken spirit dries up the bones."*

Life is beautiful and you cannot afford to live the down life. Life is yours to live! Feel on top of the world and recreate the system that drives the progress of human race. Do not observe the lying vanities, look on the bright side of life. You are not ordinary, and you cannot afford to disappoint your generation. You are beautiful, you are powerful, you are fruitful! You are full of increased wealth. You are the pride of womanhood and the C.E.O of your life, home and family.

You are wonderful, original, marvelous, adorable and note-worthy. Take your place in your marriage and do things that put smiles on the faces of your children and husband.

Proverbs 31:28 [AMP] *"Her children rise up and call her blessed (happy, fortunate, and to be envied); and her husband boasts of and praises her, [saying],"*

Life is beautiful and your marriage is beautiful, learn to laugh with your husband and not at him. Be humble, patient, show mercy, desire righteousness, have a pure heart and empower others to have a fruitful and lasting relationship. Learn not to be in temper, perfect your temperament. You know a godly wife does not get angry like a fool, in fact you do not manifest strong displeasure or bad temper. It is maturity to laugh when you feel hot under the collar or mad as a hornet.

Build trust and be loyal to your husband always! Nothing pleases a man in marriage than getting the drift and hang of the fact that his wife whom he loves can be trusted. No man wants to live with a wife that nags and nurtures her pride in the negative. Just like the way you wear clothes, your husband wants to wear your trust. He wants to be confident at all times and set the stage for the future, knowing that you will always be there for him and your children.

Song of Solomon 6:2, 3 [MSG] *"Never mind. My lover is already on his way to his garden, to browse among the flowers, touching the colors and forms. I am my lover's and my lover is mine. He caresses the sweet-smelling flowers."*

Be absolutely honest with your husband and be totally committed to the Lord.

Proverbs 31:30 [HCSB] *"Charm is deceptive and beauty is fleeting, but a woman who fears the LORD will be praised."*

Love your husband and the Lord with what it takes. Beautify yourself with the uniqueness of the love that is at work in you. Make your husband to feel special in every relevant occasion. Be sincere to your better-half and sincerely tell him how much you love him. Support him endlessly and contribute more to your husband's success than any other factor. Always make your husband to feel important without exception, and do not take him for granted.

Song of Solomon 1:7 [AMP] *"[Addressing her shepherd, she said] Tell me, O you whom my soul loves, where you pasture your flock, where you make it lie down at noon. For why should I [as I think of you] be as a veiled one straying beside the flocks of your companions?"*

Be a godly wife because no one wants to be with an ungodly woman, *"It is better to dwell in a corner of the housetop [on the flat oriental roof, exposed to all kinds of weather] than in a house shared with a nagging, quarrelsome, and faultfinding woman."* (**Proverbs 21:9**) "Better to live on the corner of a roof than to share a house with a nagging wife." (**Proverbs 25:24 HCSB**). Take up your duty and be distinctively different.

CHAPTER FIVE

HAVING GODLY CHILDREN

God wants you to have a child or children who will glorify Him. In Chapter two of this life-giving book, I made known to you that a godly home is an atmosphere of reverence and love where you, your spouse and family live in God's holy arena; making the Word of God your delight and rule of your duty. In God's holy arena, having a child or children who know how to glorify God is something that is worth living for.

All children are a gift and come from God, *"Behold children are a heritage from the Lord, the fruit of the womb a reward. As arrows are in the hand of a warrior, so are the children of one's youth. Happy, blessed, and fortunate is the man whose quiver is filled with them! They will not be put to shame when they speak with their adversaries [in gatherings] at the [city's] gate."* (**Psalm 127:3-5 AMP**)

Having a Godly child or children is a life you can

live. Yes, you can reverently and worshipfully fear the Lord.

Psalm 128 [MSG] *"All you who fear GOD, how blessed you are! how happily you walk on his smooth straight road! You worked hard and deserve all you've got coming. Enjoy the blessing! Revel in the goodness! Your wife will bear children as a vine bears grapes, your household lush as a vineyard, The children around your table as fresh and promising as young olive shoots. Stand in awe of God's Yes. Oh, how he blesses the one who fears GOD! Enjoy the good life in Jerusalem every day of your life. And enjoy your grandchildren. Peace to Israel!"*

It is important for you, especially as the head of your family to know that God wants children to be conceived and born of couples who fear and revere Him and who will bring them up under His guidance and direction. In essence, God seeks Godly children.

Malachi 2:15 [NLT] *"Didn't the LORD make you one with your wife? In body and spirit you are his. And what* *does he want? Godly children from your union. So guard your heart; remain loyal to the wife of your youth."*

As you can see, the Almighty God does not want you, me or any of His children to just have children, but to bear Godly children. Godly children can only be born from the union of Godly people. Did you understand that? There is a reason why God wants us to conceive Godly children. He wants children who will be raised in a Godly home by parents who reverence and fear Him in view of the fact that they will grow to become God-fearing men and women whom He will continue to use for His glory. This is exactly what God intended when He said to the man He created, "be fruitful and multiply."

Genesis 1:28 [KJV] *"And God blessed them, and God said unto them, Be fruitful, and multiply, and replenish the earth, and subdue it: and have dominion over the fish of the sea, and over the fowl of the air, and over every living thing that moveth upon the earth."*

When you read the Scripture as quoted above, God

starts by saying "be fruitful" and then goes on to say "and multiply." In essence, God intended for you to first be fruitful or productive so that you can reproduce your productiveness.

What a blessed assurance, the Bible also says, *"He will love you and bless you and multiply you; He will also bless the fruit of your womb…"* (**Deuteronomy 7:13**), *"Blessed shall be the fruit of your body."* (**Deuteronomy 28:4**)

God has made you fruitful, He has multiplied you. It is therefore in your best interest to reproduce your fruitfulness. Wouldn't you rather be fruitful and reproduce what God wants?

At this point someone may want to ask what exactly does God want? God wants you to marry a Godly spouse, be faithful to your spouse and give birth to children who are Godly; in other words, children of God.

Malachi 2:15 [GW] *"Didn't God make you one? Your flesh and spirit belong to him. And what does the same God* *look for but godly descendants? So be careful not to be unfaithful to the wife of your youth."*

God has given you the ability and it is your responsibility to develop the capacity you need to have Godly children! This includes being faithful to your spouse. Being married for over seven years without a child does not give you the right to cheat on your spouse. You must learn how to work your faith and thrive on the promises of God. You must learn how to connect with your spouse spirit, soul and body.

God created you in His image and likeness. God made you fruitful; yes, God multiplied you. You have received working miracles for your life and in your marriage. You have been established on the path of righteousness, peace and joy; you are establishing excellence in your marriage. Life is spiritual! Miracles take place in an atmosphere of joy! It is your responsibility to be fruitful on view of the fact that God has made you fruitful. It takes walking in the

Word of God to create the needed joy. Learning to be forgivers and givers is very important in having Godly children.

Mark 11:25 *"And when ye stand praying, forgive, if ye have ought against any: that your Father also which is in heaven may forgive you your trespasses."*

Forgiveness is very vital in marriage and having Godly children. Children are heritage from the Lord. It is the Lord that gives children. Child-bearing is not in the hands of the Lord; God puts reproduction in creation! If a Godly man meets his Godly wife at the right time, the Godly woman will get pregnant and give birth to a Godly child or Godly children.

For example, a Godly woman has twenty-eight days in her cycle, and she menstruates for the first four days. She has her fertility days between the 11th day and the 16th day. If her Godly man meets with her during these fertility days when she is ovulating, she will get pregnant and give birth to a Godly child or children.

God is not sitting in Heaven controlling babies! Child-bearing is a natural process. You may ask, can God interfere with nature? Yes; that is the supernatural; it is called a Miracle!

It requires wisdom to make things happen for you in marriage; God is not to be blamed. It is your responsibility to get the drift and hang of the fact that marriage is a place and a Godly home is a place also. And you must be powerfully placed! It is in your place to believe in God and be Godly. It is in your place to marry a Godly spouse. It is in your place to call forth your Godly children even when they are not there. It is in your place as a Godly man to meet with your Godly wife at the right time and produce Godly children.

Having Godly children is not a mystery, it starts with you understanding who you really are and believing in God. You are a special being; Be alive unto God. It is very vital to know that you are responsible for having your Godly children; you must come to a level of conviction where you know how to call your Godly children into being and speak forth the Word of God upon their lives.

It does not matter what you are seeing right now, learn to see things with the eyes of faith in marriage especially when it comes to having Godly children. Be wise to pray before getting your Godly wife pregnant; lay spiritual root before conception. Through knowledge shall the just be delivered. The Spirit and the Word of God must first have their place. Learn to take charge; work miracles and control things from the Spirit.

You are doing well. You are having Godly children, *"...Have faith in God."* (**Mark 11:22**). Give yourself to the Word of God, *"...Faith cometh by hearing, and hearing by the Word of God."* (**Romans 10:17**)

Every time you hear God's Word especially regarding having Godly children, faith comes to you in the Word. Your spirit becomes energized. Faith is not in the realm of the physical senses; it's an attribute of the human spirit. It was imparted to your spirit when you were born again. Thus every time you hear the Word of God, it goes through your mind into your spirit, for it is designed for your spirit.

Now, when you receive the Word into your spirit, that Word is more real in your spirit than the physical things that your senses perceive in view of the fact that the Word of God is also spiritual. So, if the Bible says that faith is the evidence of the things we don't see or perceive with our senses, then faith is the evidence of what the Word says! Faith accepts and exalts what the Word says above the natural circumstances of life. Therefore, faith is that response that your spirit has towards the Word of God.

Genesis 18:10 *"And he said, I will certainly return unto thee according to the time of life; and, lo, Sarah thy wife shall have a son. And Sarah heard it in the tent door, which was behind him."*

If you follow this account voraciously, you will observe that Abraham did not consider his old age but he had faith in the Word of God. Abraham believed the Word of God and God honoured His Word upon his wife, Sarah, *"And the LORD visited Sarah as he had said, and the LORD did unto Sarah as he had spoken. For Sarah conceived, and bare Abraham a son in his old age, at the set time of which God has spoken to him."*(**Genesis 21:1-2**)

Your set time to have Godly children is now. It is vital for you to regularly study and meditate on the Word. There's a spiritual reaction that is ignited between your spirit and the Word of God that gives you dominion over the circumstances of life! When that reaction takes place, faith rises in you like a giant and you have the assurance that you can have Godly children. The challenges of this world will fade away as you find yourself relating with the realities of the Kingdom.

One of the realities of the Kingdom is you can have Godly children. It does not matter what you are experiencing right now, take a leap on the Word of

God. Believe you have the needed supply, and meet your Godly wife at the right time. You have the basis and assurance for action. Do not limit yourself anymore. Speak life into your wife's womb and have your reward. Release that Godly sperm into your wife's body and have a Godly seed.

Faith is active! Activate your action and increase grace upon your life to get your wife in a beautifully family way. When your wife carries your seed, speak the life of God into that seed of greatness in your wife's womb and cause it to bear fruit of greatness.

Do not be like those who say "whatever will be, will be." Get to work and act accordingly with the Word of God. Speak forth the Word of God upon your unborn child. Call him or her names of greatness. Declare that he or she is the head and not the tail. Declare that your Godly child and children are world-changers, impact-makers, world overcomers; preachers and ministers of the Gospel.

Remember, "...*What things soever ye desire, when ye*

pray, believe that ye receive them, and ye shall have them." (**Mark 11:24**). Spend quality time and speak in other tongues. Prophesy over the lives of your children.

You are a child of Abraham *"Know ye therefore that they which are of faith, the same are the children of Abraham."*(**Galatians 3:7**). Take the faith way and have your Godly children. If God did it for Abraham, He will do it for you because you are his seed *"Now to Abraham and his seed were the promises made. He saith not, And to seeds, as of many; but as of one, And to thy seed, which is Christ."* (**Galatians 3:16**). You are an heir of God, a joint heir with Christ, a co-inheritor of the Abrahamic blessings. You are blessed to be a blessing. Go ahead and call forth your heirs.

CHAPTER SIX

TAKING UP YOUR DUTY
AS PARENTS TOWARDS YOUR CHILDREN

Every Godly parent has a duty; a moral, legal, mental and spiritual accountability that enables the children to become trustworthy and Godly. As parents, we all want the best for our children, and the best we can ever give them would have to be God's way. God's way is the only way to do it in a Godly home. Every parent has responsibilities and is under an obligation to provide for the children; it is therefore very important for every parent to take up his or her duty towards his or her children.

It is in the best interest of every parent to take up his or her duty towards the children.

Deuteronomy 4:9-10 *"Only take heed to thyself, and keep thy soul diligently, lest thou forget the things which thine eyes have seen, and lest they depart from thy heart all the* *days of thy life: but teach them thy sons, and thy sons' sons; Specially the day that thou stoodest before the LORD thy God in Horeb, when the LORD said unto me, Gather me the people together, and I will make them hear my words, that they may learn to fear me all the days that they shall live upon the earth, and that they may teach their children."*

The duties given to parents toward their children no doubt are God-given responsibilities for every household, especially a Godly home. God has a will for all mankind, He has a way in which He desires us to live our lives and how He wants us to direct the lives of our children. As a Godly parent, you must be able to nurture your children by seeking divine guidance through God's Word for the bringing up of your children.

Joshua 24:15 *"And if it seem evil unto you to serve the LORD, choose you this day whom ye will serve; whether the gods which your fathers served that were on the other side of the flood, or the gods of the Amorites, in whose land ye* *dwell: but as for me and my house, we will serve the LORD."*

You can only proclaim the authority in the above scripture when you have taken up your duty as parents towards your children. And the way to do it is through God's Word. Godly instruction is the responsibility of the parents. Parents ought to position themselves towards training their children with the Word and to do whatever they can do beyond the realm of possibilities for them to generate love and respect for God in their children.

The first way for parents to take up their duty towards their children is to uphold the whole council of God in the home. Parents must first of all put into practice the requirements placed upon them.

1 Timothy 4:12 *"Let no man despise thy youth; but be thou an example of the believers, in word, in conversation, in charity, in spirit, in faith, in purity."*

Matthew 5:16 *"Let your light so shine before men, that* *they may see your good works, and glorify your Father which is in heaven."*

In a Godly home, parents must teach their children God's way especially through leading by example. As a parent, if you expect your children to ever respect God, you must first show them how much you love and respect Him.

In order for our children to be well-trained and Godly, they must be reared in homes where the father loves and appreciates the mother. *"Husbands love your wives, just as Christ loved the church and gave Himself for it."* (**Ephesians 5:25**)

Young men are going to look to their dads to see how they are expected to be husbands and fathers, and girls will look to dad for respect and acceptance. Infact, girls who have a good relationship with their fathers, prove to marry later in life and, live the good and Godly life.

Children must see that mum and dad, although they

disagree at times and they have moments where they want to be alone, truly love one another. How we treat each other, the respect we show, will filter down through the family cell and affect young impressionable minds more than we can imagine. A Godly home should be a home where the children grow; looking up to their parents as examples of Godly parents.

For the mother, it is equally important for the children to see that she loves and respects the father. *"Wives submit to your own husbands." (**Ephesians 5:22**).* The dad is the spiritual and physical head of the home, and the mother must reflect that he is and that she respects his God-given authority, enough to let him lead. In a Godly home, the wife may give her opinion but should leave the husband room to make the final decision.

Girls will look up to mum to see how they should be as wives, and mothers must be conscious of this. The Godly home should be one where the parents show love, understanding, helpfulness, discipline and appreciation for the children. The Godly home is a place where you experience divinity at work in humanity.

Parents must take up the duty of teaching their children the dignity and reward of honest living. Training must begin in the Godly home while the children are small. As a parent, it is in your best interest to train your future hopefuls by letting them help you, even if it means the job takes twice as long or the job is not up to regular standard.

Make work fun, make it rewarding, have special treats which the children will gain at the end of the task at hand. Do not let the child shirk responsibility to escape work, teach them that they should stick it out till the end, teach them that this is how to gain satisfaction for a job well done. If you put effort in early, you will be proud of them in the future, and they will be thankful.

Praise, love and understanding are very important in

a Godly home. In a Godly home, children have the right to a Godly instruction. They have the right to an education. They have the right to be loved. They have the right to be praised. They have the right to our time. They have the right to be listened to. They have the right to learn of God and to learn the Word of God. We must love our children enough to always seek the best for them. In a Godly home, Godly children can be sweet fragrance to the Godly parents.

Children go to school but a Godly home is a divine school where the children live. In this school, the father is the teacher, under Christ. In this school, the parents must teach their children the value of the soul, of their spirit and fill them with the Holy Spirit. As parents, God's truth must govern our hearts, our dedication to God Almighty must not be superficial but heart-full and in full devotion, so that our children will follow our lifestyle in Christ.

It is therefore in our best interest as parents to present out bodies a living sacrifice, holy and acceptable to

God, which is our reasonable service.

Romans 12:1-2 *"I beseech you therefore, brethren, by the mercies of God, that ye present your bodies a living sacrifice, holy, acceptable unto God, which is your reasonable service. And be not conformed to this world: but be ye transformed by the renewing of your mind, that ye may prove what is that good, and acceptable, and perfect, will of God."*

The Word of God must be the foundation on which the home is run, with God's truth reigning as supreme. We must love our children enough to encourage their relationship with God. Children are a God-given blessing and a responsibility to us, parents. Let us not neglect such a great responsibility, nor rob our children of the best life, God's life in a Godly home. We must be able to say like Joshua stated *"but as for me and my house, we will serve the LORD." (**Joshua 24:15**)*

Wouldn't you rather serve the LORD with your

household? You have a home, fill your home with the God-Atmosphere. There is nowhere the power of divine love is so truly manifested as in a sincere Godly home. There is nothing so refreshing and full of blessings like living in God's holy arena; making the Word of God your delight and rule of your duty. A Godly home is that atmosphere of reverence and love where you, your spouse and family live in God's holy arena. That is the place we live a life that reverently and worshipfully fear the Lord.

Psalm 128:1-4 *"Blessed is every one that feareth the LORD; that walketh in his ways. For thou shalt eat the labour of thine hands: happy shalt thou be, and it shall be well with thee. Thy wife shall be as a fruitful vine by the sides of thine house: thy children like olive plants round about thy table. Behold, that thus shall the man be blessed that feareth the LORD."*

I know you are imagining how your wife will be like a fruitful vine within your house and your sons live olive shoots around your table. Relax, it is within the realm of possibility. It is very easy for your sons (and daughters) to be like olive shoots around your table if you do what you ought to do. It is in your best interest as parents to really take good care of your children. You must take good care of the gorgeous gifts God has committed into your hands. If you fail to take up your duty as a parent towards your children in a Godly home, the Bible describes you as worse than an infidel.

1 Timothy 5:8 *"But if any provide not for his own, and specially for those of his own house, he hath denied the faith, and is worse than an infidel."*

It is in the best interest of parents to take up their duties and take care of their children. Remember, children are heritage from the Lord, the fruit of the womb a reward (*Psalm 127:3*). A reward is a gift you get after you have worked very hard. Imagine receiving a reward yearly at the international stage, you will graciously and industriously make use of every legitimate means to secure and ensure that your children live healthy and remain in perfect health.

I brought that explanation to help you understand that this duty is a lifestyle that goes beyond the realm of calling. It is a kind of life you have been called to live. Apart from the joy that comes from taking care of your children, you will observe that there is this deep fulfilment when you see that your children are healthy. Good health is a great blessing especially in a Godly family. As a Godly couple, when your children are healthy, you can preach the Gospel with all it takes and without any distractions. Good health is what you get when you do things the right way. Even God Almighty understands the importance as He said *"I wish above all things that thou prosper, even as thy soul prospers."* (*3 John 2*)

Why would you be careless over your Godly and gorgeous gifts? Why would you treat your children the wrong way and destroy their soul when you can take very good care of them and prosper at the same time. By God's grace, I am happily married and greatly blessed with three gorgeous gifts from the Lord and I am enjoying the blessings of God in my Godly home. I truly take very good care of my children and therefore live this principle; prospering on every side.

I urge you parents to take the health of your children very serious. If you want to prosper; if you really value your children's happiness, and a pleasant, happy Godly home, you must take up your duty towards your children especially ensuring that they live a healthy and happy life.

In a Godly home, children deserve attention. Learn to give attention to your children. Remember your children are heritage from the Lord and gorgeous gifts to you. The easiest way to win your children's love and obedience is to give them your attention.

It is important to know that for the health of your children, your own prosperity and the overall well-being of your home, you need to exercise patience in dealing with your little *"olive plants,"* Let patience have her perfect work, be perfect and take charge graciously! Activate much of redeeming grace! Be calm and kind at the same time; you need it when it comes to training your *"fruit of the womb."*

You deserve great joy and God's grace is sufficient unto you. Teach your children the Word of God. Give them mental, moral and spiritual training. Educate your children as well as you can! It is a duty you owe to them and to God. The unvarnished truth is God will bless you and reward you in all your efforts in this direction.

Knowing that there is a reward for training your young hopefuls the Godly way should motivate you to take up your duty toward training and raising your children. It is wisdom to train your child and children, knowing that there is a reward for you. When you train your child the Godly way, you do not just a Godly way, your child grows up making the world a better place through the instructions and training you have given to him.

Proverbs 22:6 [MSG] *"Point your kids in the right direction—when they're old they won't be lost."*

The wisdom has been given to you in this masterpiece, it is in your best interest to establish the understanding you need to train your children God's way.

CHAPTER SEVEN

TAKING UP YOUR DUTY AS CHILDREN TOWARDS YOUR PARENTS

Accrding to Merriam Webster, a child is a young person especially between infancy and youth. We can simply say that children are young people between infancy and youth. These beautiful beings have conduct due to them. They have obligatory tasks, conduct, service or functions that arise from their position. For instance, children have their place in the home especially in a Godly home. In the original decision of God, children should be a blessing to their parents.

Ephesians 6:1-3 *"Children, obey your parents in the Lord: for this is right. Honour thy father and mother; which is the first commandment with promise; That it may be well with thee, and thou mayest live long on the earth."*

Exodus 20:12 *"Honor your father and your mother, that*

your days may be prolonged in the land which the LORD your God gives you."

Colossians 3:20-21 *"Children, be obedient to your parents in all things, for this is well-pleasing to the Lord. Fathers, do not exasperate your children, so that they will not lose heart."*

Proverbs 27:11 *"My son, be wise, and make my heart glad."*

Proverbs 15:20 *"A wise son makes a glad father."*

Proverbs 23:24-25 *"The father of the righteous shall greatly rejoice and he who begets a wise child shall have joy of him. Your father and your mother shall be glad, and she that bare you shall rejoice."*

You will observe from the above verses of the Bible that it is the wisdom of children to make their parents rejoice. It is in the best interest of children to seek wisdom and understanding.

Proverbs 24:3 *"Through skilful {and} godly wisdom is a house (a life, a home, a family) built; and by understanding*

it is established [on a sound and good foundation]."
(**AMP**)

Proverbs 4:7 *"Wisdom is the principal thing; therefore get wisdom: and with all thy getting get understanding."*

Children need wisdom and understanding to take up their duty toward their parents. As a child, you need wisdom to carry out your duty. Wisdom is the principal thing you need and the fear of God is the beginning of wisdom. At this point, I want you to know that the highest honour you can give to your lovely parents is to honour and obey God.

Deuteronomy 30:2 *"And shalt return unto the LORD thy God, and shalt obey his voice according to all that I command thee this day, thou and thy children, with all thine heart, and with all thy soul;"*

Ecclesiastes 12:1 *"Remember now thy Creator in the days of thy youth, while the evil days come not, nor the years draw nigh, when thou shalt say, I have no pleasure in them;"*

It is your duty to respect and honour your parents. You must have a humble subjection to the authority and control, with a readiness to perform what they require you to do.

Exodus 20:12 *"Honour thy father and thy mother: that thy days may be long upon the land which the LORD thy God giveth thee."*

Ephesians 6:2 *"Honour thy father and mother; which is the first commandment with promise;"*

In a Godly home, children must have faith in God and learn to be faithful at the same time. They should adhere to the instruction of their parents.

Proverbs 1:8,9 *"My son, hear the instruction of thy father, and forsake not the law of thy mother: For they shall be an ornament of grace unto thy head, and chains about thy neck."*

Proverbs 4:1 *"Hear, ye children, the instruction of a father, and attend to know understanding."*

Proverbs 6:20 *"My son, keep thy father's commandment,*

and forsake not the law of thy mother:"

Children should know that it is right to obey and wrong to disobey. Obedience is more than a word, it is an action that activates an operative and appropriate disposition in children. it is proper for children to obey.

Ephesians 6:1 *"Children, obey your parents in the Lord: for this is right."*

Colossians 3:20 *"Children, obey your parents in all things: for this is well pleasing unto the Lord."*

Children have the duty to honour and respect their parents. This is, of course, the essence of the fifth commandment. The principle embedded in this commandment goes beyond familial duties. The disposition of children toward parents goes beyond the realm of duties in the family. There is an honour that must be preserved. Children must give honour to their parents at all times. In other words, they must possess a lifestyle that connotes valuing highly and revering their parents.

Leviticus 19:3,14 *"Ye shall fear every man his mother, and his father, and keep my sabbaths: I am the LORD your God. Thou shalt not curse the deaf, nor put a stumblingblock before the blind, but shalt fear thy God: I am the LORD."*

The disposition of a Godly child is a combination of love and fear which moves the child to obedience. Obedience is a life every child has been called to live actively and passively. It is important for you as a child to know that true reverence results in an earnest desire to behave yourself in everything you do with a view toward pleasing your parents. You must show this honour in a respectful attitude toward your parents. You should speak reverently of your parents both in their presence and absence. You do not call your parents by their names. No, you do not do that! You are to speak respectfully to your parents. You can call your parents *"Daddy and Mummy."* You can answer them with titles such as *"Sir and Ma."* You do not answer your parents *"Yes"* when they call you. .

Good examples of Godly people who recognize the dignity of their parents are as follows:

- Isaac (*Genesis 22:7*)
- Jacob (*Genesis 27:18*)
- David (*1 Samuel 24:8; 26:18*)
- Solomon (*1 Kings 2:30*)
- Rachel (*Genesis 31:35*)

You too can obey and honour your parents. It is in your best interest to obey your parents because when you do, the obedience is *"in the Lord."* (*Ephesians 6:1*) Isaac obeyed the command of his father Abraham even when he was bound to the altar ready to be sacrificed. It is important for you to listen to the counsel of your father and mother.

Proverbs 1:8 *"My son, hear the instruction of thy father, and forsake not the law of thy mother:"*

A wise child will seek the counsel of his parents in his education, vocation, finances, and more especially in marriage prospects. No matter how old a child gets, he does not have the right to speak to his parents anyhow. A child must speak to his parents with respect. It matters how you behave towards your parents.

Leviticus 19:32 *"Thou shalt rise up before the hoary head, and honour the face of the old man, and fear thy God: I am the LORD."*

1 Kings 2:19 *"Bathsheba therefore went unto king Solomon, to speak unto him for Adonijah. And the king rose up to meet her, and bowed himself unto her, and sat down on his throne, and caused a seat to be set for the king's mother; and she sat on his right hand."*

Genesis 46:29 *"And Joseph made ready his chariot, and went up to meet Israel his father, to Goshen, and presented himself unto him; and he fell on his neck, and wept on his neck a good while."*

Speak to your parents with respect and conduct yourself respectfully before them. It is wisdom to submit to their authority and heartily comply with all their commands. Seek your parents' prayers for blessings, and be a child that brings joy to their hearts.

Proverbs 30:17 *"The eye that mocketh at his father, and despiseth to obey his mother, the ravens of the valley shall pick it out, and the young eagles shall eat it."*

Love for your parents' joy should move you to listen to them carefully. Your parents have authority over you and their spiritual teachings to you are worth more than years of self-work. It is in your best interest to listen to your parents and perform their commands. You should obey as the centurion's men (*Matthew 8:9*). There are lots of examples in the Bible you can follow. They are as follows:

- Samuel (*1 Samuel 3:5-8*)
- David (*1 Samuel 16:12; 17:17,20*)
- Jacob and Joseph (*Genesis 28:5; 37:14; 42:2-3*)
- Isaac (*Genesis 22:6*)
- The Rechabites (*Jeremiah 35:8-19*)
- Abraham's children (*Genesis 18:19*)

- Solomon (*1 Kings 2:3; 3:3, 1 Chronicles 22:11*)

As you grow in a Godly home, be prudent in your dealings and your ways. Be reasonable in your obedience in accordance with the Word of God.

Naturally, parents have more experience, ability, and a right to rule their children than the children themselves. Therefore, as a child, you cannot spend money without your parents' consent, you cannot keep friends who do not agree with your parents or who your parents do not like. And it is in your best interest to dress in a way that does not bring shame to your parents.

As you grow up, seek your parents' advice especially in the area of career and marriage. Allow your parents to guide you graciously. Your parents should guide you in this, as the examples of David and the children of Jonadab prove (*1 Samuel 16:11, 19; 17:17, Jeremiah 35*). It is your duty to follow your parents' footsteps. Your parents are wiser than you, more objective than you and you need them especially when it comes to getting married. There are examples in this regard which you can learn from. They are as follows:

- Isaac and Jacob (*Genesis 24:6-7, 63-67; 28:1-3; 29:11, 18-19*)

- Ruth (*Ruth 2:21-23; 3:1-6, 18*)

- Ishmael and Samson (*Genesis 21:21; Judges 14:2*)

- Tamar and Shechem (*2 Samuel 13:13, Genesis 34:11-12*)

As you grow up, it is an act of disparagement to take a wife against your father's will in a Godly home. On the other hand, it is a form of stealing to take away someone's daughter in the name of marriage without her father's consent. Getting married is the most important decision you will make in your life; how can you leave your parents out of it? At this point, I want you to know that though you do not have the right to choose a partner for yourself without your parents' consent, you do have the right to refuse one chosen for you, and this you must do in accordance with the Word of God.

A Godly home is a place where things must be done the right way. It is a place of respect and reverence, a place of obedience and optimism, a place of honour and higher-living. Follow the good examples of your parents. Make your parents rejoice and follow them as they follow Christ.

Proverbs 23:26 *"My son, give me thine heart, and let thine eyes observe my ways."*

1 Corinthians 11:1 *"Be ye followers of me, even as I also am of Christ."*

Examples of people who followed good examples in the Bible are as follows: Solomon, Asa and Timothy (*1 Kings 3:3, 2 Kings 22:2, 1 Kings 15:11, 2 Timothy 1:5*)

As your parents grow older, it is your responsibility to care of them. It is wrong to assume that the state will take care of your parents at their old age. It is your wisdom to serve them more than they served you in view of the fact that you owe your parents so much. Show gratitude for their kindness and supply of your needs. Be eager to repay their provision in any way that you can. The smallest thing you can do is to acknowledge their parental love and care.

A Godly home is a spiritual place where love and care are perfected. Piety must begin at home by showing your appreciation to your parents. Learn to make your parents happy and preserve their good name. Honour your parents as much as you can. Obedience to parents is not an arbitrary thing, but a solemn divine commandment with the greatest reward. Obedience to your parents is the best motive possible for anything. The Lord vigorously enforces the fifth commandment.

Ephesians 6:1-3 *"Children, obey your parents in the Lord: for this is right. Honour thy father and mother; which is the first commandment with promise; That it may be well with thee, and thou mayest live long on the earth."*

Take up your duty towards your parents and obey them in all things acceptable to the Lord.

Ephesians 6:5-6 *"Servants, be obedient to them that are your masters according to the flesh, with fear and trembling, in singleness of your heart, as unto Christ; Not with eyeservice, as menpleasers; but as the servants of Christ, doing the will of God from the heart;"*

Colossians 3:22-23 *"Servants, obey in all things your masters according to the flesh; not with eyeservice, as menpleasers; but in singleness of heart, fearing God; And whatsoever ye do, do it heartily, as to the Lord, and not unto men;"*

CHAPTER EIGHT

BUILDING A

STRONG FAMILY BOND

Building a strong, united home is every parent's desire. The bond of a family lasts a lifetime and parents can help build a firm foundation. Our family teaches us how to function in the system that drives the progress of humanity. The family should provide love and warmth to all its members. A strong family gives its members the support they need to make it in life.

Happy families have strong family bonds. In a Godly home, parents have to be responsible for building, strengthening and protecting the family bond. Building a family bond does not happen naturally, it does not just happen. You are the one to call it into being. You can create this firm foundation by committing yourself towards building a strong family bond.

Building a family bond is a lifestyle we can live, and understanding the concept of family will really help us to build this strong bond. The concept of family is extremely important in the Bible, both in a physical sense and otherwise. The concept of family was introduced in the very beginning as we see in **Genesis 1:28 [NIV]**, *"God blessed them and said to them, "Be fruitful and increase in number; fill the earth and subdue it. Rule over the fish in the sea and the birds in the sky and over every living creature that moves on the ground."*

God`s plan for creation was for men and women to marry and have children. A man and a woman would form a *"One flesh"* union through marriage, *"Therefore shall a man leave his father and his mother, and shall cleave unto his wife: and they shall be one flesh."* (*Genesis 2:24*) and they with their children become a family, the essential building block of humanity and our society.

The bond of a strong family is very important and it is therefore in our best interest to build a bond that will make a great and Godly family. Every family should first of all have a vital relationship with God Almighty who created them and offers them the power to live a life of joy and purpose.

Jesus Christ said, *"I came that they might have life, and have it abundantly."* And Psalm 16:11 tells us that in God's presence is *"fullness of joy."* God gives us a biblical plan for building our family strongly.

In every family, the members must understand that it is impossible to build a strong family bond when each and every one of them is yet to put Christ on the throne of their lives. When family members put Christ on the throne of their lives, they yield to God's control. This family's interests are directed by the Holy Spirit, resulting in harmony with God's plan and strengthen their bond as a family.

Galatians 5:22-23 *"But the fruit of the Spirit is love, joy, peace, longsuffering, gentleness, goodness, faith, Meekness, temperance: against such there is no law."*

The God's Word Translation and Amplified Translations put it this way.

Galatians 5:22-23 [GW] *"But the spiritual nature produces love, joy, peace, patience, kindness, goodness, faithfulness, gentleness, and self-control. There are no laws against things like that."*

Galatians 5:22-23 [AMP] *"But the fruit of the [Holy] Spirit [the work which His presence within accomplishes] is love, joy (gladness), peace, patience (an even temper, forbearance), kindness, goodness (benevolence), faithfulness, Gentleness (meekness, humility), self-control (self-restraint, continence). Against such things there is no law [that can bring a charge]."*

It is beautiful to live a life of purpose, power and plenty; living in God's plan. It is important for us to take to heart that in a Godly home, strengthening your family bond strongly is an important way of life we must embrace. When parents build a strong family bond, they set a Godly stage for the children to do the same in the future.

Happy and Godly families have strong family bonds. Parents have the responsibility to strengthen and protect these great bonds. Building a strong family bond is something parent can do; it is a lifestyle every parent must live. In building a strong family bond, you must understand that the timing must be right. Take a look at everyone's schedule; try to make a regular night. May be once a week, when the entire family gets together for a fun activity. By keeping it on a regular schedule, everyone will know that they need to keep that night clear for family times. If you are going to plan a day trip, try to do it at least one month in advance. Post it on the family calendar and make sure that adults and teens are aware of the plan so they do not make other plans.

Building a strong family bond is a way of life that

includes eating meal together as a family. I understand that members of the family may have different activities on daily basis, resulting in them leaving the home at different times. But a family that wants to really build a strong family bond must eat together as a family as often as they can. Apart from helping members to bond together as a family, it builds confidence in family members to do well in life and live a healthy life.

Every family has a value and this value comes into place when building a strong family bond. Create a family mission statement that works! A family mission statement can remind every family member about each other. It is simple and fun to develop as a family. Place your mission statement in a predominant place in your home. Read it and talk about it often.

For example when a family has a mission statement that includes *"We're Special to God."* This creates a consciousness on the mind of every member of the family.

1 John 3:2 *"Beloved, now are we the sons of God, and it doth not yet appear what we shall be: but we know that, when he shall appear, we shall be like him; for we shall see him as he is."*

When this family prays to God, knowing how special and precious they are before God. They do not have any sense or act of self devaluation. They know they are a Godly home and they have received Christ and believed on His name.

John 1:12 *"But as many as received him, to them gave he power to become the sons of God, even to them that believe on his name:"*

Family members have strong bond and they know they are special to God. They know that God reproduces after His own kind. They know they are the crown of God`s creation, the best of all He`s made, created in His image and likeness. They know they look exactly like Him. They know it is impossible for a dog to give birth to a monkey; neither can a cow beget s human. They know God only gives birth to His very kind. They know Lord Jesus has brought them into oneness with charge of the entire creation to reign and rule over all things.

Nothing moves a Godly home with a strong family bond where the members know who they really are in Christ. They are bold to declare that they are God's special possession; His specially crafted masterpiece called by His Name, and made in His image and likeness. They are conscious of their real personality! They know they are royal diadem, peculiar treasure, kings and priests of God. They know they have been chosen to lead their generations. They know they are holy nation, God's own specially crafted and divinely created family; born to proclaim the praises of Him who called them out of darkness into His marvelous light. Yes, they live conscious of their oneness with the Father and the special place of glory, virtue and honour that they occupy in Him.

You too can boldly say you are special to God. Yes, as a parent, you can build a strong family bond and inculcate in family mission statement that *"We Belong to Christ."* It does not matter what your family used to be. I want you to know that the *"you"* that existed before, ceased to live. The life of the old *"you"* was supplanted with God`s divine life.

You have a duty and a call to teach your family members this truth. Do family responsibilities together, have family meetings and encourage support for each other. Encourage and inspire your family members to totally surrender their lives to Christ. Make them to understand that they cease to live a carefree life from that moment in view of the fact that they`ve given Christ the right to rule and reign over their lives. Empower them to know that they must forthwith give Him the right of way to have the final say in all their affairs.

Colossians 3:4 *"When Christ, who is our life, shall appear, then shall ye also appear with him in glory."*

When you as a parent have achieved this, you give your family members a higher life and commissioned them onto achieving the reality of a strong family bond. There is so much you can do together as a family. Learn to study the Word of God together and make a success of your lives.

Joshua 1:8 [TLB] *"Constantly remind the people about these laws, and you yourself must think about them every day and every night so that you will be sure to obey all of them. For only then will you succeed."*

Make it a duty to plan things and projects together. Come up with great ideas and create something new. Be it vacations, chores or after school activities, make your plans together as a family. There is nothing wrong with including your kids in your planning. Share the ownership of whatever you are doing with them; always remember they are part of you. Learn to read together and go on vacations together also. Other beautiful ways to create strong family bond is to cook the dinner together, have scheduled family movie nights, have scheduled family game day/nights, make the very best of resources and go to Church as a family and possibly sit together. You can build a strong family bond and a Godly home; loving each other. Start with the Word time.

CHAPTER NINE

LIVING GOD'S PURPOSE

Every one was born with a purpose! You were born with a purpose and it is not an accident you have a life, home and family.

Ecclesiastes 3:1 [AMP] *"To everything there is a season, and a time for every matter or purpose under heaven:"*

Years ago you were born on this earth, you went through the stages of education, got involved in different activities, did different projects, executed different strategies, and in this day and age, you have a home. God gave you a home for a purpose and that purpose is God's purpose. It is important for you to know that no one came into this world without a God-given purpose.

2 Timothy 1:9 [AMP] *"[For it is He] Who delivered and saved us and called us with a calling in itself holy and leading to holiness [to a life of consecration, a vocation of* *holiness]; [He did it] not because of anything of merit that we have done, but because of and to further His own purpose and grace (unmerited favor) which was given us in Christ Jesus before the world began [eternal ages ago]."*

God has a plan for you and your household! He has given you the grace to live His purpose for you and your family. Just take a look at your abilities, there is something about you that is not ordinary. There is more to you than who you think you are. Take a great look at your spouse, there is so much to your spouse than you can ever imagine. Take quality time to study your children, you will notice that these gorgeous gifts from God are beyond the capacity of your imaginations.

God has a plan for you! God has a unique plan for your life, home and family, different from that of any other living person. There is nobody like you and there is no home like your home. It is an error to compare your home to another home. God created you and empowered you with gifts, talents and abilities to have a home that is out of this world. His plans and purposes for your life are distinct, in view of the fact that He doesn't have, has never had, and will never have a carbon copy of you.

You are and extraordinary! You are beautiful and powerful, and your home is God's best. In **Romans 11:29 [AMP],** the Bible says *"For God's gifts and His call are irrevocable. [He never withdraws them when once they are given, and He does not change His mind about those to whom He gives His grace or to whom He sends His call."* The Message Bible Translation puts it this way *"God's gifts and God's call are under full warranty— never canceled, never rescinded."* WOW! What an assurance for you and your home. It is therefore your responsibility and that of your household to build a godly home. It is in your place to make your home a place where the Word is the rule of duty and duty a delight that fulfils God's vision.

It does not matter what you have known life to be or what culture you have been exposed to, place your life before God, *"So here's what I want you to do, God helping you: Take your everyday, ordinary life—your sleeping, eating, going-to-work, and walking-around life— and place it before God as an offering. Embracing what God does for you is the best thing you can do for him. Don't become so well-adjusted to your culture that you fit into it without even thinking. Instead, fix your attention on God. You'll be changed from the inside out. Readily recognize what he wants from you, and quickly respond to it. Unlike the culture around you, always dragging you down to its level of immaturity, God brings the best out of you, develops well-formed maturity in you."* (**Romans 12:1, 2 MSG**).

Lots of people and homes settle for a kind of life, a level of life where they live their own vision for their lives, society's vision for their lives and even the devil's vision for their lives. Most of them may experience great life and success but in the end, they lack fulfilment, satisfaction and peace of mind.

Proverbs 19:21 [AMP] *"Many plans are in a man's*

mind, but it is the Lord's purpose for him that will stand."

The good news is that you bring the best out of you. God develops well-formed maturity in you when you live His great purpose for your life, home and family. You are here on earth for a purpose and that purpose is God's purpose.

God created you in His image and likeness! You are God's best and beloved. It is important for you to know that God has predestined your life for glory; He has destined you, according to His purpose, for a specific assignment. You were born for a purpose; God put you on earth for a season; there is a definite purpose for your life, home and family. Therefore, no member of your home and family should drift along in life, without any sense of purpose. It is very important for you, and every member of your home and family to discover your purpose and their purpose in life.

Imagine the fulfilment, satisfaction and peace of mind that comes from building a godly home where the

Word of God is the firm and good foundation. Imagine going out to preach the Gospel to the people on the street and giving lives a new meaning with your spouse and children. What a life of joy and fulfilment of purpose.

Jesus was on earth for a specific purpose and He wasn't in doubt as to what that purpose was. In John 10:10, He established His purpose: "… *I am come that they might have life, and that they might have it more abundantly.*" He knew He didn't just come to the world to look around and breathe his last. No, His life was not meant to be an uninspiring life; His whole life was in pursuit of a purpose to save and give life to all men.

In John 20:21, the Lord said, "… *Peace be unto you: as my Father hath sent me, even so send I you.*" This is your purpose now and that of your home and family. You've been sent to reach all men with the Gospel of life. The day you gave your heart to Christ, He gave you His kind of thinking and made you a saviour just like Him. The day you got married, you entered into an institution that belongs to God Himself. You do not have your own right anymore, you live your right in Christ.

You and your home have what it takes to live God's purpose. You and your family really have to be passionate about the enthronement of God's Kingdom in the hearts of men, and its expansion to the ends of the earth. Learn to talk to someone about Christ as you embark on that trip. Speak to someone about the beautiful life in Christ as you execute that business. Encourage your spouse to be wise and win at least a soul for Christ. Teach your children to win their mates at school for Christ.

Remember that God does not withdraw His gifts and call from you and He does not have any plan of replacing you or your family with anyone because He has given you His grace. He has given you and your home the grace to excel.

2 Corinthians 9:8 [AMP] *"And God is able to make all*

grace (every favor and earthly blessing) come to you in abundance, so that you may always and under all circumstances and whatever the need be self-sufficient [possessing enough to require no aid or support and furnished in abundance for every good work and charitable donation]."

You and every member of your home have the grace to excel in everything including living your God-given purpose. God is able to direct all the grace you and your family require for anything in this life towards you and your household, such that you're never lacking in ability. God has given you the ability and it is in your best interest to develop your capacity in view of the fact that you have all the competencies and special skills required for excellence in living your God-given purpose. The same applies to every member of your home and family.

Yes you can! Yes your home can. The ability of God has been made available to you and your house. No wonder Paul the Apostle declares in **Philippians 4:13**

"I can do all things though Christ which strengtheneth me."

No one can stop you from living your God-given purpose. It is your right in Christ to live a fulfilling life, do not try to stop yourself. You and your house have been specially enabled to live God's purpose. This explains why you must build a Godly home; a place of sufficiency and ability where you refuse to function with your human ability but function with divine might because you know you are God's masterpiece. You and your household are very special and important to God and that's why He chose and made you His best.

Ephesians 2:10 [AMP] *"For we are God's [own] handiwork (His workmanship), recreated in Christ Jesus, [born anew] that we may do those good works which God predestined (planned beforehand) for us [taking paths which He prepared ahead of time], that we should walk in them [living the good life which He prearranged and made ready for us to live]."*

You and your family are God's best and His most cherished workmanship. God has predestined your life and that of your family for glory. He has pre-ordained your life, home and family according to His purpose, for a specific assignment. It behoves you and your family, as children of God, to locate yourselves in that divine plan. And this starts with building a Godly home.

I want you to know that you don't go around looking for God's purpose for your life and that of your home; you learn it! You give yourself and your home to studying the Word; it is not something you do by chance or accidentally.

It is in your place and that of your household to make up your mind to fulfil God's purpose in your lives. Locate yourself in God's plan, and decide that you and your home and family will fulfil God's purpose for your lives. God's purpose is God's destiny for your lives. It's your responsibility to ensure that you walk in the path that He's prepared for you, your home and your family.

Colossians 4:17 [AMP] *"And say to Archippus, See that you discharge carefully [the duties of] the ministry and fulfill the stewardship which you have received in the Lord."*

From the above Scripture, you observe that the Apostle Paul giving a very vital admonition to a certain man named Archippus, to take heed to the ministry, which he had received in the Lord, so that he (*Archippus*) may fulfil it; he didn't say that God might fulfil it for him.

If you look at the above paragraph closely, you will notice that then Apostle Paul was admonishing Archippus, he said to him, to take heed to the ministry, which he had received in the Lord. He didn't say to him to take heed to the ministry, which he had received from the Lord. This is a calling you do in the Lord and not away from Him.

You can have a Godly home and fulfil God's purpose

in your life, home and family. Yes you can! You and your family can live in God's destiny for you and follow His plan for your lives, just learn and give yourself to the Word; have a good knowledge and understanding of God's Word.

Proverbs 20:5 [AMP] *"Counsel in the heart of man is like water in a deep well, but a man of understanding draws it out."*

God's purpose is hidden in your heart; it is deep inside the recesses of your heart and you have the Word of God in your life. That right Word for the right purpose, for the right time and for the right you.

Remember, the Word of God is near thee, even in your mouth *"But what does it say? The Word (God's message in Christ) is near you, on your lips and in your heart; that is, the Word (the message, the basis and object) of faith which we preach,"* (**Romans 10:8**). God has given you His Wisdom! He has also given you His Light to locate His purpose for you, your home and family.

Proverbs 1:20-24 [MSG] *"Lady Wisdom goes out in the street and shouts. At the town center she makes her speech. In the middle of the traffic she takes her stand. At the busiest corner she calls out: "Simpletons! How long will you wallow in ignorance? Cynics! How long will you feed your cynicism? Idiots! How long will you refuse to learn? About face! I can revise your life. Look, I'm ready to pour out my spirit on you; I'm ready to tell you all I know. As it is, I've called, but you've turned a deaf ear; I've reached out to you, but you've ignored me."*

Psalm 119:130 *"The entrance of thy words giveth light; it giveth understanding unto the simple."*

All you need is a good understanding of the Word of God in view of the fact that every purpose is established by counsel.

According to **Proverbs 20:5 [AMP]**, *"Counsel in the heart of man is like water in a deep well..."* You will agree with me that if you stand before a well, you see yourself. This lets you know that the Word of God is your mirror and all you need to do is locate yourself in the Word and draw out your God-given purpose from deep within your heart.

Study and meditate on the Word of God so that you will receive insight, direction, and be guided rightly to make choices and decisions that are in sync with God's plan for your life, home and family.

Joshua 1:8 *"This book of the law shall not depart out of thy mouth; but thou shalt meditate therein day and night, that thou mayest observe to do according to all that is written therein: for then thou shalt make thy way prosperous, and then thou shalt have good success."*

Learn how to yield yourself and members of your household to the Holy Spirit, through constant fellowship. This is very important for you to understand the mysteries and divine secrets that will help you discover yourself in God's dream.

You, your home and family are not ordinary! Psalms 139:14 says you're *"...fearfully and wonderfully made ..."* You're one of a kind; a creation of complexity and wonder, not easily explained; that's what you and your family are. You are God's best!

1 Peter 2:9 *"But ye are a chosen generation, a royal priesthood, an holy nation, a peculiar people; that ye should shew forth the praises of him who hath called you out of darkness into his marvellous light;"*

You and your home have a God-ordained purpose to illuminate your world with the light of God and be a blessing to your world. God wants you to bless your world. He has called you and me, and your household to the ministry of reconciliation.

2 Corinthians 5:19 *"To wit, that God was in Christ, reconciling the world unto himself, not imputing their trespasses unto them; and hath committed unto us the word of reconciliation."*

1 Corinthians 1:9 *"God is faithful, by whom ye were called unto the fellowship of his Son Jesus Christ our Lord."*

God has committed to you and your family the

ministry or reconciliation; not only did He call you into the fellowship of His Son Jesus, He's also called you to partner with Him in soul winning. Have you seen the most important reason why your home must be a Godly home? It is in your best interest and that of your family to illuminate your world with the light of God because the whole world is waiting for you and your home to manifest His grace.

Romans 8:19 *"For the earnest expectation of the creature waiteth for the manifestation of the sons of God."*

Matthew 5:16 *"Let your light so shine before men, that they may see your good works, and glorify your Father which is in heaven."*

You must live God's purpose and bless your world! You must win for others. Don't allow the victory of Jesus over sin, death and the devil to be in vain. Jesus won for you *"And God sent me before you to preserve you a posterity in the earth, and to save your lives by a great deliverance."* (**Genesis 45:7**). Let lives be saved, transformed and preserved because of you and your family. You were born into greatness, *"For as many of you as have been baptized into Christ have put on Christ. There is neither Jew nor Greek, there is neither bond nor free, there is neither male nor female: for ye are all one in Christ Jesus. And if ye be Christ's, then are ye Abraham's seed, and heirs according to the promise."* (**Galatians 3:27-29**).

Build a Godly home, live God's purpose and make things happen in this life and be like your Father, *"Great is the LORD, and greatly to be praised; and his greatness is unsearchable."* (**Psalm 145:3**). Build a Godly home today and reign greatly! Greatness abides in you even now.

ABOUT THE AUTHOR

Monique **Chika Kalu** is a World Renowned Marriage Mender, Relationship Expert, Marriage Counsellor. She is the co-host of first-class and success-filled Marriage is Beautiful Couples' Banquet, Marriage is Beautiful Gala and Marriage is Beautiful Couples' Retreat which takes place in Nigeria, USA, UAE etc.

She is married to **Kalu Igwe Kalu**, President & CEO of *Marriage is Beautiful Foundation*, an organization that has impacted millions of individuals and families online and real time through their seminars, conferences and Marriage is Beautiful Online Platforms. She speaks favor and victory daily to over 8 million online followers and call out their seeds of greatness. Her marriage is blessed with three lovely Children.

ABOUT THE BOOK

Building a Godly home is a lifestyle that reverences God and manifests love for the Almighty God. It is a way of life where one pursues right standing with God and true goodness; having the loving fear of God and Christlike, and living a life of prosperity

In this mind-blowing and life-changing masterpiece, *Building a Godly Home, Monique Chika Kalu* teaches you what Godly home is, how to find and marry a godly spouse, how to take up your duty as a Godly husband or wife, how to have Godly children, how parents and children should take up responsibilities towards each other, how to build a strong family bond and fulfill God`s purpose.

This reality will empower you with what it takes to build a Godly home and create the perfect bond of unity among the family members to accomplish God`s vision and be totally fulfilled.

www.ingramcontent.com/pod-product-compliance
Lightning Source LLC
LaVergne TN
LVHW041320080426
835513LV00008B/530